CHILD OF MANY RIVERS

CHILD OF MANY RIVERS

Journeys to and from the Rio Grande

LUCY FISCHER-WEST

TEXAS TECH UNIVERSITY PRESS

Photos of the author taken in India
are by Bob Entrop, Philip Menicucci, and Mark Steffen.
All photos are from the author's collection.

This book is typeset in Monotype Dante.
The paper used in this book meets the minimum
requirements of ANSI / NISO Z39.48-1992 (R1997).
∞

Designed by Mark McGarry, Texas Type & Book Works

Printed in the United States of America

Library of Congress Cataloging-in-Publication Data
Fischer-West, Lucy, 1949–
Child of many rivers : journeys to and from the
Rio Grande / Lucy Fischer-West.
p. cm.
Includes index.
ISBN 0-89672-556-1   ISBN-13 978-089672-556-0
1. Fischer-West, Lucy, 1949– 2. El Paso (Tex.)—Biography.
3. Ciudad Juárez (Mexico) —Biography. I. Title.
CT275.F5584A3 2005
976.4'96063'092—dc22
2005008806

05 06 07 08 09 10 11 12 13 / 9 8 7 6 5 4 3 2 1
SB

Texas Tech University Press
Box 41037
Lubbock, Texas 79409-1037 USA
800.832.4042
ttup@ttu.edu
www.ttup.ttu.edu

For you who love
and inspire me

CONTENTS

THE GIFT OF CULTURE
A FOREWORD

Those of us who live on La Frontera, the border between México and the United States, who have been raised by parents who appreciated the power of all cultures, and who continue to celebrate our border world with its rich diversity of peoples, languages, and dreams—we understand, or should, the immense privilege bestowed upon us.

Culture is a precious gift, not to be taken lightly. But to understand what culture really means, one must explore the nature of one's growing up and the life blood of home and family. Moreover, one must study the deeper implications of lessons offered by those we come from, most particularly our parents and other relatives who can teach us who we really are. If we shun these lessons, we are children bereft of sustaining roots.

In my travels as a writer and educator, I encounter people of all ages, whose deepest common desire is to belong to someone, something, to be connected to family and to be embraced unconditionally by that family, no matter their heritage or background.

Few people, if any, want true separateness from their heritage. And even those who do can never truly deny their ancestors, for they carry in their very being the pulse of that life source. What good then can come of running from self? Most of us turn intuitively from this denial.

In Oklahoma, a young Mexicana adopted into an Anglo family confided that her adoptive parents forbade her to date Mexicanos or any Latinos. This, she knew, was a negation of who she was, and naturally she found it deeply troubling.

Likewise, I have met others who knew they had Native American blood, but Grandfather (or Grandmother) wouldn't speak about it, nor would he (or she) let anyone in the family speak about or celebrate their ancestry. This silence, born of misplaced shame or some misguided intention to protect, is our American tragedy.

The history of American-born Mexican-Americans is full of the sad stories of children punished for speaking Spanish in the school yards and, conversely, of parents who, fearful of the consequences, refused to speak Spanish to their children. Only now do many Mexican-Americans understand the tragedy of assimilation at all costs. Sadly, they must struggle to discover their cultural heritage and often cannot communicate in their grandmothers' or grandfathers' native tongue.

I remember my grandmother, Lupe Triviz Chávez, interrogating those who came into her daughter's Elisa's house, "¿Quién te parió?" Who gave you birth, or more formally, from whom are you descended? Who are your people? Once she received the needed information that so and so came from the Gómez or Contreras clan from over there in Rincón or Doña Ana, and was a cousin of a cousin of La Señora Montoya's whose father was from Hatch, the family coming from Juárez during the Revolution, all was well with my Grandma Lupe. If things were only so simple now.

If our world was smaller when we were growing up, we can only imagine how much smaller, and in some ways more enviable, was the prescribed world of our Frontera parents, who knew who lived where and where they came from.

Things have changed dramatically. Yet as we combine into a wonderful and vital mestizaje of cultures and backgrounds, languages and mores, ways of being, doing and creating, we must realize that we are children of many borders. How rich our world is now, too, as men and women travel as never before and connect to each other through the various media that bring sound, light, color, and image to us at the twinkling of an eye.

The purpose of a book about family is to create family. And this is what Lucy Fischer-West has done in her memoir, *Child of Many Rivers*.

In the course of introducing us to her German father, Martin Franz Jockisch, the name later changed to Fischer, and her Mexican mother, Lucina Lara Rey, Lucy shares the gift of their lives, their stories, their deep bond of love, a love that transcended borders both literal and symbolic. How often have such scenarios played out in the world, unsung and under-celebrated?

The story of the Fischer family is one story of our frontera, the borderland region. Lucy Fischer grew up with the shadow of la muralla / the wall, symbolic and as real as the chain links of the fence only yards from her house. Lucy shows us the powerful reality of the border, a place that holds joy and sorrow, tradition and newness, complexity and simplicity.

In those days, the muralla was not so pronounced. Like Lucy and her mother, we didn't see its shadow or feel its darkness as deeply as we do now. People went back and forth more naturally between México and the United States, and depending on where you lived, the crossing was easy.

In my mother's hometown of Redford, Texas, just across the river from Ojinaga, México, people crossed the river without fear of reprisal. The crossing, necessitated by the daily machinations of life, was often made in a chalupa, or canoe, with foodstuffs or lumber in the boat, because that was what you needed on the other side.

Now the muralla in Nogales is made from recycled materials from Desert Storm, and in Tijuana it's a concertina-wired wall that slides into the water—if you wanted to cross, you would have to swim far out into the water to get away from the wall, but who would do that? Only the most foolhardy would swim that far out to reach the American side of the water.

One has but to see the disparity of "this side and that side" to reflect deeply on what culture really is and how our human-made boundaries are something we need to look at deeply, to reassess and to reevaluate.

How do we live in a world that perpetuates the myth that we are separate from each other? How can we think that what affects one does not affect another, especially in our border corridor where people are dying every day merely in hope of seeking a better, more hopeful life? The American Dream, as envisioned by the Fischer family, seems more elusive every day.

I have reflected on the power of work in the lives of Martin and Lucina Fischer and marvel at their endurance, strength of spirit, and abiding hope for a better world. Their story is not only the story of a man and a woman; it is a story of how to live in the world. And their success, which became their daughter's, can be ours as well.

I applaud the work Lucy Fischer-West has done in *Child of Many Rivers*. She has written with a clear conscience of heart and from the deepest place of understanding about her parents, two distinct and larger-than-life forces of nature, who connected, made a life, and out of that union produced a true daughter of la frontera. The gift her parents gave her was the understanding that through love, all disagreements, all injustices, all so-called boundaries and misunderstandings between people can be worked through, if not totally eradicated. Martin and Lucina prove how deep thought and understanding can erase *fear* from our vocabulary. It is fear that holds us back from embracing those we perceive as different or strange and that robs us of respect and dignity, which after all, is what every sentient being—man, woman, or child—wants. And this is the kind of family that *Child of Many Rivers* delights in and shows us so concretely.

The Fischers, Martin and Lucina, deserve their own book, as they are the impetus of this story of home. Theirs is a complex tale and broad, full of unexpected commonalities that lie just beneath the web of so-called difference. What wonderful people they were! And this is brought to life so vividly and with such love by their daughter.

We are all children of many rivers. We must never forget that. In this troubled and scarred world of perceived differences, books like *Child of Many Rivers* offer us the best of hope, faith, and joy in who we are, what we can become.

As I write this, the New Year is upon us. Can we make peace with our family? And if we can, what stops us from making peace with ourselves and anyone else?

May *Child of Many Rivers* live a long and prosperous life, bringing waters of understanding to all who read it, nurturing us and sustaining us with its wisdom and grace.

DENISE CHÁVEZ
Las Cruces, New Mexico

UN MILLÓN DE GRACIAS

The knowledge, kindness, generosity, and love of those who have made this work possible make my soul sing with gratitude. To Judith Keeling, my editor, who heard my voice and had the vision and perseverance to make it appear on these printed pages, you have moved me to tears with your faith. To Lucina Lara Rey and Martin Frank Fischer, my parents, who gave me life and made it beautiful, how I wish you could hold this book in your hands. To John Martin West, my son, a far better wordmaster than I, a powerful influence in my life, thank you for the pen with which these stories were written. To Meredith E. Abarca, Professor Miffy, who champions my every act of agency, I'm glad you came when you did and live so close. To Skip Clark, who years ago with his unselfish sharing of postcards opened up a floodgate of El Paso–Juárez memories, your love of local history is contagious. To the strong women who believe in me, day in, day out—Ruth Vise and April Vise. And to Mary Beth Harper, the kind of friend who would come at 3:00 a.m. if I needed her. To Art Delgado, who helps keep me healthy, to Daniel Chacón, who insisted on stories to go with his meals, and to Lex Williford for his always kind and gracious words about my writing—your friendships make my life so rich. To John O., who sustained himself on pimento cheese sandwiches and Oreos and milk while this was being written. To Bob Esch, whose red pen bled all over my first college essays, I hope I remembered enough of what you taught me that you'll not need too much ink now. To James M. Day, who taught me so much more than how to research, edit, and index, and who kept my cars from falling apart for so many years. To Doc Sonnichsen, who in so many letters told me I should write what I know. To Melvin P. Straus, whose vast knowledge of the era in which my father came to America helped me write his story. To Gordon S. Bowie and Elma Devlin, who with their families cared for me in Scotland. To Paulette Dupré, friend, mentor, second mother, you are a bright light in my life. To the Rotary Foundation, which gave me India. What an incredible gift. To the men and women of the Texas Folklore Society, who have taken me in and embraced me with their encouragement. To Joyce Gibson Roach, who coaxed light out from under the bushel basket where it had been hiding for years. To Francis E. Abernethy, who liked what I wrote enough to publish it. To Amit Ghosh of *BorderSenses* and Elaine Davenport of Writer's AudioShop, who have also given my voice an audience. To those who worked with me at Texas Tech University Press: Barbara Werden for invaluable assistance with the photographs; Lindsay Starr for a cover design so rich and beautiful; Katherine Dennis for so patiently shepherding this work from its beginning to what you now hold in your hands; and Courtney Burkholder for helping my story find its market. I could never thank you enough.

CHILD OF MANY RIVERS

PROLOGUE

I GREW UP believing I was a child of this river, the Rio Grande, *el Río Bravo*, the bold, wild, restless. Its nature complemented my own. It was, after all, the Rio Grande that brought my parents together, wrought their destined border union and, for that matter, me. Theirs was a marriage of constancy not without commotion, with a rhythm like the river's, sometimes serene, sometimes impetuous.

Yet looking back, I see that other rivers were tributary to this story. On Germany's River Elbe was the harbor from which my father left in 1912 to seek his fortune. My mother, many years younger than he, drew strength from the Chihuahuan *Río Conchos* of her birthplace. Conceived on the banks of the Rio Grande, I traveled in her womb across America to New York, to be born alongside the colder waters of the Hudson, in Catskill. I was still an infant when the Rio Grande and the culture so deeply embedded in my mother called the two of us back, to the river's Mexican side, until my father retrieved us. He took us across the river again, to settle for good in *El Paso del Norte*. There, on the border, they raised me, an only child, a fortunate child, for going back and forth across this river taught me much. I took root on the river's banks; there I grew up, married, reared my own child, and laid both parents to rest. My mother left me her sense of the holiness of rivers; my father, his sailor's wanderlust. These bequests took me east, past the ocean that carried my father here, to Scotland's River Clyde, then west, where on a California bus I met a soul kindred to my mother's, who led me to French rivers dear to her. Then came India and the Sacred River Ganges. This, then, is a story of many rivers, rivers that seem to me now ever connecting, ever offering new chapters.

LUCY FISCHER-WEST
On the banks of the Rio Grande,
January 2005

MY FATHER THE SAILOR

MY FATHER had the most beautiful light blue eyes in the whole world. I suppose every dark-eyed child with a blue-eyed father would say the same, but I know it to be so. They shone with a long lifetime of journeys. They twinkled with clownlike merry-making. They held secrets he never imparted. It makes me sad that a life so fully lived cannot be fully told. He was a gentleman and a gentle man who never raised his voice, a quiet philosopher. When I asked what he'd done, where he'd been, what adventures he'd had throughout his world travels, he would skirt the query with "Ask me no questions, I'll tell you no lies." Whatever juicy tidbits there were in his life before Lucina, my mother, he never revealed them.

As I write, I have before me a black metal box, no bigger than a small clutch purse. It holds one family photograph, certificates in German I cannot read, two passports, several union member-ship cards, some immigration documents, a handful of ornate but worthless stock certificates from Steele's Consolidated, two letters of recommendation, and a few pages in my father's hand-writing recording the places he visited on dates decades before my birth. The contents of this box are all I have to construct my father's life before he came to Texas. Those papers, two cassette tapes too brittle and delicate to play, a few edge-worn photos too big to fit in the box, the few stories he did share, and recollections of my time with him are what I have to tell his story. Tucked inside a silk-covered, embroidered photo album from Shanghai is a picture of him looking rather sheepish, seated with another sailor while a Chinese soldier, standing ramrod straight, seems to be keeping watch over both of them. It remains one mystery picture I will never figure out. To say that I need more facts and details to keep his memory alive would be inaccurate. But oh how I would love to know every secret, every place he ever went, all the things he did before he settled down to be my father.

Lucy's father, left, in his Merchant
Marine uniform, in Shanghai, China, in 1946.

He was born August 22, 1891, in Harburg, Germany, and christened Martin Franz Jockisch. His siblings were Bertha, four years
older; Karl, two years younger; and Martha, who was five years
younger and lived only until she was twenty-three and pregnant,
a victim of the 1918 influenza epidemic. He went to elementary
school in an era when students were caned not only for misbehavior but also for giving the wrong answer to a question. About
1903 he graduated from elementary school and for the next two
years worked on a dairy farm in Rheindorf, moving up from
apprentice to dairyhand status when he could milk twenty cows a
day, twice a day. From 1906 to 1907, he worked first in a rubber
factory, then a comb factory in Hamburg, both of which he hated
because he had to be indoors. By 1909 he had joined the German
navy, which broke his mother's heart, he said. He left for his initial assignment from the harbor at the River Elbe, going to signal-
man's school in Wilhelmshaben for three months, then on to the
North Sea at Nordsee for coast guard duty. Judging by the only
picture I have from those years, my father was fit and trim, with
an athletic body. To pass the time of day, he strung a rope across
two posts on the porch of the house he shared with two other
men and taught himself how to walk a slack rope. Evidently he
got bored with the assignment after about three months and,
early in 1912, requested a transfer to the German fishing fleet,
where he cast nets for halibut and cod in the North Sea and the
North Atlantic. While at sea, he slashed his hand severely enough
that he was sent to a hospital onshore.

At the hospital he met a Russian sailor who filled my father's
head with tales of America—America, he said, where anyone
with a desire to work hard could become wealthy, where opportunities were plentiful. That was the place to go. The Russian said
it was easy to jump ship in New York City; he knew lots of people who had done it. And besides, he warned, if my father went

The Jockisch family, circa 1912 before Lucy's father left Germany.
Seated, from left to right: Martha Henschel Jockisch, Franz Josef Jockisch,
Karl Jockisch. Standing, from left to right: Martha Jockisch, Martin Franz
Jockisch (Lucy's father), Bertha Jockisch.

back on a fishing ship, they would go farther and farther north as
the season wore on. The increased cold would heighten the risk
of losing his injured hand. The years my father was in the German navy, all ships, regardless of their function, were part of the
fleet, so there were other assignments he could seek. His new
duties put him on the *Königin Lüise,* a huge new passenger vessel
going to America. There were 2,000 immigrants on the ship,
nine-tenths of whom were from Poland and Russia, the eastern
countries. Some spoke German. They paid $40 to $50 for a one-to-
two-week trip across the Atlantic, bedding down in a room
crammed with open bunks and buckets for latrines. They were all
on the way to what they hoped would be a better life. For my
father, it was the sheer adventure that was appealing, a new start,
something exciting. One night the steersman got drunk and

couldn't do his job. Even though he had never served as a steersman, my father volunteered and managed to impress the officers with his abilities. That was one story he was fond of telling. Officially, he was a steerage steward on that voyage across the Atlantic, serving meals to passengers and cleaning up after them, the latter a most putrid task since many missed the buckets.

On December 11, 1912, he arrived in New York City, slung his loaded seabag over his shoulder—which isn't very wise if you're planning a surreptitious exit—and started down the ramp. An alert guard sent him back. My father must have acquired some smarts overnight, because the next day he settled for putting on all the layers of clothes he could manage and left everything else behind; he picked a time when a different guard was on watch and waltzed off the ship with no difficulty. Twenty-five dollars would have allowed him to enter the country legally, but he had less than five when he arrived. Besides, he was the daring sort, liking a challenge.

It was the dead of winter. He knew no one, spoke not a word of English, had no place to go. He picked a Central Park bench for his first night's accommodation, with newspapers fished out of the trash serving for both mattress and blankets. That is how my father started his life in America. On the ship he had read about a Lutheran mission that was supposed to help immigrants. He found it, but also found that it was a place where the military police came regularly, looking for deserters. For those sailors caught, the punishment was six weeks in confinement, feet and hands shackled to a chain that ran from the floor where it was anchored, between one's legs, and up to a cuff around the neck. He didn't stay long at the mission. Back to the park bench he went. After a few days of the bone-chilling cold, he got up his courage and picked out a policeman with a friendly face and asked him where he might find cheap lodging. The policeman took my father to a boarding house run by a Bohemian woman who spoke German. The cost was $2 a week; my father had $1.90 in his pocket. She took him in anyway.

According to the classifieds he had read in a New York-printed German newspaper while on the ship, there were plentiful jobs for immigrants, but if you couldn't speak English, there were only two: dishwashing or window washing. Since it was winter, he decided on the dishwashing. Besides, he was sharp enough to figure out that if he found a job in a restaurant, he would at least get one meal a day. The restaurant that hired him paid him $7 a week for seven twelve-hour days, with two meals a day thrown in. Out of his first week's seven dollars, he used six for a month's worth of English lessons in night school.

You may be wondering whether this is going to be a Horatio Alger story, an only-in-America rags-to-riches story. It's not—at least not in terms of material wealth. My father's measure of success was acquisition of knowledge. Just as I remember his "ask me no questions" quip, I remember his motto that man should always strive not to "have more, but to be more." In his mind, to "be more" involved books, an education. When he tired of his mostly Polish coworkers in the kitchen deliberately mispronouncing his surname, Jockisch, as "jackass," he tried pearl diving—a then-common euphemism for dishwashing—elsewhere for three months. Even as an illegal alien, my father always had a job and a place to sleep. Whenever possible, he took jobs that offered food as well as pay.

His next job took him out of New York City. He hired out to one of the East Coast railroads and became a gandy dancer, so named for the tools from the Gandy Manufacturing Company in Chicago and for the fact that stepping back and forth over the ties placed at intervals longer than a normal stride created a sort of dance. The railroad provided food and shelter—in the railroad cars—while the men worked repairing sections of track. His aim was not to work for the railroad indefinitely but to make it to Cleveland, Ohio, where, it was rumored, half the population spoke German. He had gone on the gandy dancer job with a friend who wasn't too fond of hard physical labor and lasted only a couple of days before he escaped the boxcar accommodations to continue on foot. My father stayed on the job until he made it to Cleveland.

Loving the water as he did, he got a job on a lake steamer that went from Cleveland to Buffalo, again as a dishwasher. When winter set in, he stayed in Cleveland and became a busboy—an exalted position, he said, because busboys didn't have to wash dishes. By the end of his first year in America, he was earning $12 per week, nearly twice his starting salary. He stayed there for eight months, until the restaurant changed hands and the new owner didn't want to pay him that amount, even though by that time he was experienced. For a while he worked for the railroad again, then he found a job as a short-order cook, reconnected with the restaurant owner who had treated him well, and went to Cambridge Springs, Pennsylvania, where he worked his way up to be a "black suit" waiter in a first-class hotel that catered to a Jewish clientele. He was the only German employed there.

He must have worked earnestly at being a good waiter, because one of the dog-eared books I inherited from him is entitled *The American Waiter* by John B. Goins, published in 1914 and purchased for $1.25 from the Angelica Jacket Company in New York City during his first month there. It is a comprehensive book, elucidating that a rum omelet is served on a large platter to the left of meats and that, after asking permission, waiters are to move to one side of the guest and light and burn the rum. It also specifies that Japanese persimmons are served with plate, spoon, *and* finger bowl; informs the reader that whitefish is carved differently from other fish; and provides a detailed diagram on the proper serving of Alaska Soufflé. Perhaps this attention to the proper way of handling food explains the impeccable table manners my father had. He ate in a refined European fashion, not switching the knife back and forth from one hand to another. With his fork and knife he could scrape every bit of meat off any bone and never, ever get any food on his fingers.

Then there were instructions on the proper deportment for waiters. "Never run, hop, skip or jump while at work in the dining room, but have a lively gait, swift and silent, and not calculated to attract attention." Mr. Goins ends the section on deportment with the following: "Keep out of strikes. If you are asked to join in a strike for better wages, refuse point blank. And I would advise you to offer to quit; but first explain why you do so, stating your reason for quitting is to keep out of strikes." As to the excuse that "my wife was sick, [I] had to remain to give her medicine," Mr. Goins retorts, "If your wife is sick, you come to work and earn money to pay your doctor bill and buy her medicine, for you can do her no good to remain and look at her." In capital letters at the end of Section I, among other things, he emphasizes "DON'T pull your mustache, DON'T play or get familiar with female help, DON'T make a disturbance because you are going to quit." And just in case you missed it the first time, "DON'T strike."

His employer wanted to take him back to Cleveland, to wait tables there, but told him he needed to belong to a union to do so. The waiter's union turned him down because he had not worked at least two years as a busboy, so he joined another union in Cleveland, the Ice Wagon Drivers', Chauffeurs' & Helpers' Union, Local No. 422. Until a horse stepped on his foot and left several of his toes permanently deformed, he drove an ice wagon. After that misfortune, back he went to the business of waiting tables, this time at the Peoples Restaurant, owned by one George Fleischmann, who "found him a very good worker, honest, prompt, sober and reliable," according to a letter of reference written on a half sheet of paper when my father left his employ.

In April of 1917, after Archduke Franz Ferdinand had been assassinated and the *Lusitania* had been sunk, the United States entered World War I, and my father's immigrant status changed from "illegal alien"—the term used at the time—to "enemy alien." In March 1916, while in Cleveland, he had filed a "Declaration of Intention" to become a U.S. citizen, renouncing "forever all allegiance and fidelity to any prince, potentate, state, or sovereignty, and particularly to William II, German Emperor, of whom I am now a subject." In June, he rid himself of the last name of Jockisch, which had elicited taunting on his arrival in America. For a new name he chose Martin Frank Fischer, the last name to reflect the sailor in him.

But the naturalization process went nowhere, for reasons unknown to me. Had his papers been in order, he could have joined the armed forces as he wanted and become a citizen within thirty days. He did, however, register in the Military Census and Inventory of 1917 and carried that card with him. As an enemy alien, he ran the risk of being interred for the duration of the war. I imagine his resourcefulness kept him out of the internment camps. What do you do when you suddenly find yourself on a government's list of undesirables merely because you're the wrong nationality? My guess is that you try to get lost in the crowd; you keep moving. Even better, you go on the road with the circus or a vaudeville act. The Selective Service Act of 1917 exempted entertainers from active duty. Their mission was to keep up the morale of the country. I believe that slack-rope walking and years of honing his acrobatic skills at the YMCA were what allowed him to stay in America.

The greatest treasures for me in the black metal box are fourteen yellowed notebook sheets of paper labeled "On the Road with De Perón Trio" in my father's handwriting. Those sheets document his whereabouts from January 27, 1917, to November 27, 1919. During that almost three-year period, the trio performed no fewer than 546 engagements in thirty-two of the forty-eight states. In 1918, they spent the tail end of July, all of August, and through mid-September performing with the Barnum & Bailey Circus in Kansas, Missouri, Oklahoma, Colorado, Wyoming, Utah, Idaho, Washington, Oregon, and California. I never knew the names of the Trio's other members. In what looks like a promotional picture, there is one man in mime makeup complete with a big bow around his neck and a ribbon-decorated beret; my father and another man are in leotard-type undershirts, the kind worn by acrobats. All three men are handsome, but of course my father has the most beautiful smile, the most expressive eyes. The De Perón Trio was an acrobatic comedic team, and to hear my father tell it, they were no fly-by-night performers. The fourteen pages that chart his months as an entertainer seem to back that up. The troupe's first booking was in the Haltworth Theater in Cleveland.

In flowing, dip-pen script, there are dates, the theaters where he performed, and the circuits he was on. The Gladden and Zimmerman took him to Illinois and Michigan, the Loew-Doyle to Wisconsin, the McLaughlin to Pennsylvania and Maryland, the Lowe to New York City, Boston, and Providence, and the Kauffman to Massachusetts. The Western Vaudeville Managers Association booked the trio at the Windsor Theater in Chicago. They played the Rialto in Chattanooga, Tennessee, the Victory in Charleston, South Carolina, the Priscilla in Cleveland, the Cataract in Niagara Falls, the Jamaica in Long Island, the Calumet and the California in Chicago, and a string of Electric Theaters in

St. Joseph, Joplin, and Springfield, Missouri, and Kansas City, Kansas. Right after he had worked at the Strand Theater in San Bernardino, California, in mid-October 1918, the entry reads "All theaters closed." There is no explanation as to why. The De Perón Trio's last two stints, in November, 1919, were at the Plaza Theater in Freeport, Long Island, on the Fally Marcus Circuit, and the Academy of Music in Brooklyn, on the Universal Booking Office Circuit, the outfit that booked Al Jolson in all its theaters. During his time as an acrobat, he went back and forth across the Ohio River, crossed the Mississippi several times, and spent time in the Great Lakes Region.

The end of the war marked the end of his vaudeville days. At twenty-eight, he settled back in New York City. From the end of 1919 to 1931, he was general manager of a doughnut shop on

De Perón Trio, circa 1918. Martin Fischer is on the lower left.

Seventh Ave. It is hard to believe that doughnuts were ever touted as a healthy food, but they were. For years in his room there hung an undated newspaper article about the benefits of eating doughnuts. Previously, it had graced the walls of The Cruller, one of "New York's Original Doughnut Shops" owned by William J. Carney, who had nothing but high praise for my father's efforts in his business. "Sober, honest, and industrious, a man of splendid character," he called him. My father supported himself through the Great Depression frying doughnuts and, ever the entertainer, making up singing rhymes to make the trip to the shop more interesting for customers.

About 1930, my father was encouraged to go to Canada and reenter the United States legally. With the help of his employer, who sponsored him, he did just that. He finally got his green card in July of that year, eighteen years after he had jumped ship; his certificate of citizenship is dated February 5, 1934. The same year, at the age of forty-three, he got his Evening Elementary School Certificate from the state of New York. Those documents are the only clues I have as to where he was in the early thirties. Nothing in the black metal box tells me of his whereabouts between then and the early forties. After becoming a citizen, he went back to Germany to spend several months with his sister Bertha and her family. His sister Martha had already died. His brother Karl, who had Americanized his name to Charlie, had settled in New Jersey with my father's help. Bertha had survived World War I in Hamburg. When a bombing killed her first husband, she had placed his body in a wheelbarrow and taken it to the cemetery to dig his grave herself and put him to rest.

It was not until 1943 that my father went back to sea. They took him in the U.S. Merchant Marine, even though he was a bit long in the tooth—fifty-two to be exact. His first steamship, the *Frederick Von Steuben,* took him initially to Argentina. The Merchant Marine hauled freight and war *matériel* from the mainland to wherever troops were stationed. If he had any close calls during his wartime service, he chose not to share them with me. I do know that in early June of 1944 he was docked at the River Clyde in Scotland. When the Japanese surrendered in 1945, his ship was ordered to Leyte Gulf in the Philippines, where the entire crew spent four months without shore leave, a punishment for the misbehavior of a few. The first week of January 1946, they went to Shanghai, about a week's sail away. At a private party he met a "nice Eurasian girl" named Suzi Seiter, a forty-two-year-old widow whose Welsh husband had died five years before. She had two daughters in their twenties and a thirteen-year-old son. My father and Suzi started dating, and one day in April, in a rickshaw traveling down Bubbling Well Road, she proposed to him. Suzi told him about a psychic, "a refugee Jewess from Vienna," a Madame Hahn, who had made the *Shanghai Daily News* by predicting the end of the war and other important events. Suzi wanted to ask her whether my father was destined to stay in China. Madame Hahn's words set the marriage plans awry. She told him he would have to return to the States to get his discharge from the U.S. Merchant Marine as well as his back pay. Then she added, "You are going to meet a girl in Latin America, will fall in love and marry her." Suzi was heartbroken. In May of 1946, my father's ship was ordered to leave China for the United States. They were paid off in Wilmington, California, and he was given a train ticket to New York.

He stopped in El Paso for a brief holiday because he wanted to see a bullfight across the border. Although he had traveled extensively, he had never seen one. After settling into a room at the Armed Services YMCA, he took a streetcar over the Rio Grande to Juárez on a Sunday afternoon in June. The Plaza Alberto Balderas was packed, but not with bullfight fans. Pity. He could have stumbled onto an event featuring the legendary Manolete. But I shouldn't say that. Had the tragic Manolete been the main attraction for the afternoon, I would not be telling this tale. What my father found was a Lion's Club charity fiesta and dance. Schoolteachers had been recruited as chaperones for the event, and my mother, Lucina, was one of them. He knew instantly that she was the woman that Madame Hahn had said he would meet.

In the custom of the day, the men walked clockwise in an outer circle while the women went counterclockwise in an inner circle. He spotted her first. She wore her wild, wavy black hair long in those days, and loose. Her eyes were jet black and her peals of laughter resounded as she interacted with those around her. Her movements had an elegant grace. He noticed that, too, since he had been a dancing man all his life. It took three passes around the circle before they connected, but after that, they danced exclusively with each other for the rest of the evening. They did not talk much. He had only a smattering of Spanish, and she knew no English.

He asked if he could see her again, and they set up a day and time for a date. Not knowing how my grandmother would react, my mother told him they could meet at the Oasis Restaurant in downtown El Paso, next to the Plaza Theater. By the third date, he had the engagement ring ready for her finger. He proposed, and she accepted. For the remaining days of his two-week stay at the Y, he went back and forth across the border to see her, meet her friends, and make a good impression on his future in-laws. At the end of the whirlwind courtship, he boarded a train for New York to reenlist for another two-year stint in the U.S. Merchant Marine. On whatever ship he traveled, he increased his Spanish skills in his spare time with books like *Spanish in 20 Lessons* and *Hugo's Spanish Verbs Simplified*. Needing help with his romantic correspondence, he purchased a how-to book on writing love let-ters in Spanish entitled *Cartas Amorosas*. He wrote her from all over the world and sent her gifts as well, from chocolates to exquisite Oriental dolls to jewelry: from Russia a coin necklace, from Florence an exquisite cameo, from Germany a honey-col-ored faceted amber brooch. Just to affirm that he was serious about his proposal of marriage, he wrote a letter proposing once more. It was a very formally phrased poetic missive, written on a round-cornered light cardboard sheet—the kind used inside a package of nylon stockings.

> *Will you marry me?*
> *My darling will you marry me—And share my humble life?*
> *Will you declare yourself to be—my own beloved wife?*
> *Will you be ever at my side—in sickness and in health—With*
>   *courage and with equal pride—In poverty and wealth?*
> *Will you inspire me to fame—However dark the sky?*
> *Will you do honor to my name—Until the day I die?*
> *Will you adore our children and protect them day or night—*
>   *And guide them with loving hand—To live for what is right?*
> *Then take me darling for your own—and put your faith in me—*
>   *I shall be loving you alone—For all eternity.*

My mother used to ask him who got the stockings, but he never would say.

My father came back to the border in the spring of 1948, in time to hear his bride-to-be sing at a Mother's Day program at *Centro Escolar Revolución* where she taught. If he had not already been smitten, hearing her soprano voice surely would have con-vinced him that she was talented as well as beautiful. She was also well loved by her students, so much so that some threw rocks at my father and his car when he would come to get her

Will you marry me?

My darling will you marry
me — And share my humble
life? Will you declare
yourself to be — My own
beloved wife? — Will you
be ever at my side —
In sickness and in health
— With courage and with
equal pride in poverty and
wealth? — Will you in-
spire me to fame — How-
ever dark the sky? — Will
you do honor to my
name — Until the day I
die? — Will you adore our
children and guide them
with loving hand — to live
for what is right? Then
take me darling for your
own — And put your faith

The proposal letter.

after school. I think he had imagined that the minute he showed up, she would drop everything and marry him. She said no, not until the school year ended the last week in June. She finished the school year and planned their wedding, doing the cooking for the reception herself at my grandmother's house. The *Primera Iglesia Bautista* in Juárez was filled to capacity for the nuptials. The reception was crowded as well, and she was the proper hostess, looking after everyone's needs. My father was the proper host, dancing with all the ladies there. When everyone finally left, my father was ready to begin their life together. My mother, tired and hungry, said she wasn't going anywhere until she cleaned up the mess so that my grandmother wouldn't have to. My father said OK, shrugged his shoulders, and went back to the Armed Services YMCA in El Paso. He did not come back for three days. That's how they started out their married life. When they did have a honeymoon, they took my Tía Toña with them to Chihuahua and got stuck out in the desert. The two women spent a terrifying night in his broken-down jalopy listening to the howl of the coyotes as he slept soundly.

The first few months of their married life, my parents lived in the back of my grandmother's house while my father started the proceedings for my mother to become a permanent U.S. resident. He went across the border into El Paso every day to work as a carpenter's helper on the Fort Bliss Centennial construction. In due time, at the age of thirty-eight, my mother became pregnant, but miscarried. Shortly thereafter she conceived once more and was told that if she wanted to carry the baby to full term, she must be practically bedfast for most of the nine months. My Tía Ofelia offered lodging for my parents and care for my mother in her house a few blocks from where my grandmother lived. Come May when she was six months pregnant, my father in all his wisdom decided that it was time to drive to New York State where

Lucina Lara Rey and Martin Frank Fischer,
Lucy's parents, on their wedding day. June 27, 1948.

he had a house. My aunts and grandmother begged him to wait. He declared that where the husband goes, the wife must also go.

The "house" that my father owned was a ramshackle tar-paper shack in the Catskill Mountains, a mile from Cairo, in the woods, on a hill, with no facilities of any kind and no neighbors within miles. Neighbors would not have done my mother much good, since she still spoke almost no English. She was a dutiful wife, doing all that was required of her in that wilderness setting, including carrying water up the hill from a stream off the Hudson River. I would not be surprised if she even had to chop her own wood. I consider myself a miracle baby, having survived the hardships of my mother's life during the last three months of her pregnancy. Since Cairo did not have a hospital, two weeks before my mother's due date, my father drove her to Catskill. The car died two blocks from the hospital. He did have enough sense to go get a wheelchair to take my mother the rest of the way there, but then he went on about his business. I guess he thought he had done what any good husband should do, made sure his wife would be taken care of. He was not there when I made my grand entrance into the world on August 5, 1949. True to the times, and the small-town location, my mother was kept in the hospital for two weeks. When she was preparing to leave, the staff told her that if she did not have better living conditions for me before winter set in, the state would take me and find me a home. I don't think the full impact of that statement ever reached my father's brain.

My Uncle Charlie, who came from New Jersey to meet me, had a serious talk with my mother after she related the hospital's admonition. He said that at fifty-eight, having been on his own all his life, my father was used to taking care of himself but would never be a good husband or father. He encouraged my mother to

Lucy, newly born, with her father in the Catskill Mountains.

go back to Juárez. I was less than three months old when my father drove us as far as the Albany airport door, never thinking that my mother would need help with the loads she was carrying and, given how little English she knew, that she might need help finding the right plane. He went on to find a buyer for some lots he had acquired in Ohio, bought yet another clunker, this time a truck, loaded up what possessions he chose to bring, and came to my grandmother's house to retrieve us—five months later.

After moving to El Paso, we lived first in a house on Virginia Street across from Henry Trost's El Paso High School, then later in the housing projects on Olive Street, where my father came home one summer day in 1951 and proudly announced he had bought a house. A consultation with my mother had not occurred to him. As he saw it, since he was paying for it, it was his decision to make. That was a major source of contention during my parent's marriage. He was old school: the husband was the breadwinner, the wife the homemaker, the mother. The wife did what the husband wished her to do. He had saved $2,000 and signed a note for the remaining $1,700, with payments of $30 per month at a 6 percent interest rate. He thought she would be thrilled. On her first visit to the house, located in the *Barrio del Diablo*, he declared that one room of the four-room house, which included only a partial bathroom with no bathing facilities, would be for his books. It was in that house that I got to know my father.

For the first seven years of my life, wherever we lived, he worked in construction, sometimes for the R. E. McKee Company and at other times wherever there was a job. In construction, as elsewhere, he was loyal to the local union. Work was so scarce that it was not unusual for him to work only three days a week. That my mother managed a household on such a meager income is to her credit. Whatever furniture we acquired we owed to her resourcefulness. My father's morning routine consisted of rising early and doing Walter Camp's Daily Dozen Health Building Exercises, all of which he had on 78 rpm records. He would finish with what I then thought was just an acrobatic headstand, flush against the wall, but that I later realized was part of a daily yoga meditative practice. Then he would go work a full day and come home to gather green dandelions along the median on Paisano Avenue to feed to the rabbits. He would tend to the chickens and rabbits, then read until my mother called him to supper. At bedtime my father read or sang to me in German. He also tried to teach me how to walk a slack rope, but he made the mistake of using my mother's clothesline posts to secure the ends. When she tripped over the training rope, my potential circus career came to an end.

My father never got over the Depression. He would bring home every conceivable piece of junk known to man and pile it in the yard. In time he built a shed from the scrap lumber he had gathered. After he filled the shed, he started stacking things on top. I remember a box spring on that roof. Eventually the shed caved in. That backyard fed my imagination in a way a well-kept yard might not have. Every space in that yard held something interesting for me. There were lots of chickens, mostly running around loose, and rabbits in hutches. I know we ate the chickens, but I do not remember eating the rabbits. There was one sweet, pale brown and white rabbit that was a pet. He lived a long and happy life until one day when I stupidly picked him up by the ears and he decided to reciprocate by clamping his teeth into the base of my right thumb. I cried and cried, not just in reaction to the bite but because he was hauled off somewhere while my hand was being stitched together. I suppose he had to be tested for rabies. I never knew what became of him. Most of the kids on the block, at one time or another, got baby somethings for

Easter—bunnies or chicks or ducks. And as cute little critters are wont to do, they grew up to be messy big critters. Still, I pampered my favorite duck with his own red-rimmed white enamel basin for a wading pool. My father brought home an unexpected guest one afternoon and the next thing I knew my pet duck was being served for Sunday dinner. My father explained patiently that this man could not eat whatever my mother had fixed, so being a good host, he had to improvise. I could say that the experience left me traumatized and that I've never been able to eat duck since, but that would be a lie. I love well-prepared duck.

All through my early childhood, there were two old cars in the backyard, one a 1937 Chevy. Cars in backyards were not an unusual sight in my neighborhood. Ours must not have been very dependable vehicles since we didn't seem to go very far in them. Every Sunday my father would drop off my mother and me at the *Primera Iglesia Bautista Mexicana*, and then go to the Reverend Charles Manker's Unitarian Church, of which he was a charter member. But we did not go out of town much in his jalopies, especially after we got stranded once in the desert between El Paso and Alamogordo and my mother came home exhausted from entertaining me in the fine red dirt, filling up assorted cans we unearthed. My all-time favorite childhood excursion was one to Ruidoso, New Mexico. After wading barefoot in the *Río Ruidoso* at the Upper Canyon with my mother, I spent the rest of the day with my father, first riding the ponies that were tethered to a wheel of some sort. After I tired of that, we explored the town. Hand in hand, we went all over, I in my overalls covered with hay and he looking somewhat disheveled. When it came time to go home, the car wouldn't start. The mechanic he found told him how much it would cost; he could not afford to fix it, so he sold it to the man for $25 so we would have enough for bus fare to get home. After that, if we went out of town at all, we went with my mother's friends.

I know we must have been poor as dirt, maybe more so than some families on the block, but I do not remember ever feeling like I did not have what I wanted or needed. At Christmastime, we always had a tree, and one year Santa came walking down our street in broad daylight accompanied by a photographer who offered to take my picture in our very own living room. I asked him how he was going to put presents under the tree since we did not have a real chimney he could come down. He said it wouldn't be a problem for him; he would figure something out. He did. That Christmas, I saw my father walk out the back door, then come back in the front, telling me he had found Santa, who had sent a gift for me—a yipping, hopping, black-and-white windup puppy. My father was always doing that—meeting Santa somewhere on Christmas Eve. It never occurred to me to doubt that Santa really was in the *barrio* handing out gifts for children whose houses did not have chimneys.

The day the shed roof caved in after a summer rain, I discovered other treasures in my backyard, most notably two big

Lucy at age six, with her father in Ruidoso, New Mexico.

theatrical trunks filled with an assortment of clothes belonging to my father. The clothes dated back four decades. He did not seem terribly concerned that some of them were wet and moldy. My mother saved what she could, including his silk top hat, white tie and tails, and several cotton batiste formal dress shirts with dozens of tiny tucks in the front. The cardboard collars to go with them had gotten soggy, so she threw them in the trash along with dozens of other items. It was during that rescue effort that I first saw the picture of my father and his German family dating back to before he came to America and the most wonderful picture of all—the one of him in his acrobat outfit when he performed with the De Perón Trio.

Poor as we were, my father the dreamer saw to it that I had experiences to expand my horizons. I vividly remember sitting between my parents close to the stage at Liberty Hall when I was six, watching Maria Tallchief dance in *Swan Lake* when the Ballet Russe de Monte Carlo came to town. My father's and my yearly traditions included going together to Barnum & Bailey Circus performances and the Southwest Rodeo at the Coliseum, the latter with me dressed in a red hat with white lacing around the edge and a fringed vest and skirt my mother had made for me. Every other Saturday, he and I did the rounds paying bills, and he introduced me to the El Paso Public Library, where I spent many, many hours with him. Trips to the zoo and Washington Park swimming pool in the summers were also special, until one time when he went off to do some diving and swim in the deep end and someone had to save me from drowning. Sadly, my mother put an end to those pool outings; my father was a champion swimmer, but thanks to that incident I never did learn to do much more than stay afloat.

About the time I turned eight, my father went to work in the bottleshop at the Falstaff Brewing Company. This was a steady job, five days a week along with all the beer he could drink as long as he could still do the job he was paid to do. Every two weeks his shift changed. The regular mealtimes that we had enjoyed as a family became a thing of the past; his good intentions to teach me German, at least the most elementary phrases, were put aside as well. But there was always time to read. He got me a subscription to monthly books on geography, which came with stamps to be affixed to the appropriate page. He wanted so much for me to travel, to see some of the places he had seen; the time we shared reading the books and putting the stamps in them was like being in exotic places with him. Except when he came home at 2:00 a.m., my mother had hot meals waiting for him. For those arrivals, she would leave two eggs in a saucepan and he would soft boil them for himself, capping them carefully and giving our dog Daisy the part he had cut off. Daisy's table manners had the same finesse as his. She licked every bit out, never broke the shell, and then lay at my father's feet until he went to bed.

While he worked for the brewery, there was an addition to the backyard that fueled my imagination even further: two parade-float swans that were large enough to climb into. I had ridden in one of them in the Sun Carnival Parade on the cold first day of the year right after he started his job at Falstaff. My mother made my dress, a pink tulle multiskirted creation that made me look like something that should be on top of a cake. The finishing touch to the outfit was a hooded royal blue velvet cape and long white gloves. I rode proudly on the Dinkey Bird float with the amfalula tree and the castle in the clouds. True to his habits, my father rescued the swans and brought them home. My striped orange cat and I took many a flight in those swans. They lasted until the rains of summer made them look like soaked *piñatas*.

Either we became prosperous enough not to need to raise

chickens and rabbits, or the backyard mess finally got to my mother. The animals and junk disappeared, and she put in fruit trees and a shed that wouldn't cave in and added to the few rose-bushes growing in spite of the clutter. On the day that my father took in his documents to prove that he had reached the age of sixty-five so he could retire, he astounded management with his birth certificate—he was actually seventy-five. The work that he did was heavy, strenuous labor; his coworkers were decades younger; he never had trouble keeping up. He had never missed a day of work, including the week after the Friday he fell asleep on the drive home and crashed his car into a rock wall, breaking the steering wheel with his chest. A $30 pension check came every month during the first ten years of his retirement.

Once he retired, my father had more time to dedicate to the books he had acquired throughout his lifetime. The library was diverse; there were lots of how-to books, like *How to Keep Hens for Profit* and *The Amateur Trapper,* plus astro-navigation books left over from his sailor days. Alongside those were the Harvard Classics, the works of Victor Hugo, Ralph Waldo Emerson, and Edgar Cayce. My father believed that there was a supernatural world worth exploring for its riches, that we all had telepathic, psychic powers we never developed, minds that never reached their full potential and bodies stronger than we gave them credit for; he visited the Christian Science Reading Room on a regular basis and loved the positive-thinking writings of Norman Vincent Peale, whose church he had attended while living in New York. He kept a daily journal, but never recorded the stories of his trips, which is what I would have most liked to read. It has taken me years to realize that to him journeys of the mind were more significant than the physical places he visited. As a young man in New York, he attended classes in Eastern philosophy taught by the Hindu sage Rishi Sherval, who had studied with Tibetan monks. My father thought him the wisest, purest, and noblest man he had ever met and corresponded with him for years. Believing in reincarnation, he hoped that he had lived a life that would merit a kind rebirth. And in fact, I never heard my father speak a harsh word about anyone.

My father was unfailingly supportive and proud of everything I did. I went through Zavala Elementary involved in everything—choir, plays, volunteer work—and as long as his job schedule permitted it, he attended all of my school functions. While I was attending high school at Lydia Patterson Institute, he cheered me on, applauding my every effort. Earlier he had taught me to roller-skate, and watched me get pretty darn good at it; later, he taught me how to drive our big, black, boxy, standard 1949 Plymouth. In the days when stores were not open on Sunday and the Fox Plaza Shopping Center parking lot was empty save for the spots in front of Parkins Cafeteria, I practiced under his patient instruction. I remember going around and around in circles in the lot forever before I ever drove on a real street. If a learner's permit was required, I don't think I got one. He led me through driving short distances until I got comfortable. At school during lunch, I practiced in my best friend's little Renault. I had no trouble getting my license, thanks to the parallel parking instructions I got from the friendly street-parking attendants in Juárez. Yes, I drove in Juárez, most likely before I had a license, just to make sure I could pass the test when the time came.

With me at the wheel dressed in a teal blue, floor-length organza formal, on my way to the senior Spring Fiesta, the Plymouth's transmission died. Thank goodness for girlfriends who had followed me from home to the hall after doing my makeup for the event. Otherwise, the Queen would have had to make her entrance without her Lady-in-Waiting. My father went back the next day to retrieve the car with my Uncle Tom, and together they decided it needed to be put out to pasture. (But someone rescued and restored that car. For years, my mother and I used to see it regularly on our shopping trips to the *Mercado Cuauhtémoc*.) Had I not idolized my father and thought *he* could do no wrong, I would have gotten better advice when it came time to get a car for myself. Even though he had gotten a certificate from the New York City YMCA Automotive School in 1932, he did not have a very good track record when it came to choosing cars. The honeymoon jalopy had left them stranded in the desert; the one in which he took my mother across the country gave out repeatedly; even the one in which he drove my mother to the maternity hospital didn't make it all the way. The one he picked out for me was a red 1960 Ford Falcon. In the years I owned it, the muffler fell out, the radiator blew every summer, and the transmission clunked out and left me in the middle of busy intersections at least twice. On the plus side, I became a practiced hand at tinkering with the solenoid to restart it every time it died, a technique I learned as a student assistant from my first English Department boss at Texas Western College.

Of all the things I did that made my father proud, graduating valedictorian and then going on to college were the most significant. Except for night-school classes in English, my father's own formal education had ended in the eighth grade. Yet books and learning were the driving force in his life. I was fulfilling the dream he had been unable to realize for himself. He took on the household chores that my mother thought I should do so that I could study instead. When I told him after my junior year of college that I wanted his blessing to marry a college professor, he was happy for me. At the age of seventy-nine, my father walked me down the aisle, proud as could be that I was going to be the wife of a man who valued learning as much as he did. For the next nine years John and he sat together every weekend for hours on end, talking of hardships during the Depression, of books they had both read, and of philosophy—those "verities of life" that he always told my mother he was mulling over instead of helping her with the house.

My father's sight began to fail when he hit eighty. When my mother let it slip that she had to tell him when traffic lights turned red or green, I insisted he give up driving. The State Commission for the Blind supplied him with Talking Books and he diligently continued his pursuit of knowledge, listening to book after book after book. He watched little television except in the evenings with my mother, the only time she stayed still long enough to let him rest his head in her lap. He continued to do the Walter Camp exercises and did his headstand meditation into his early eighties. He spent years proving to us that his body could heal itself through what he learned in Christian Science and yoga. He had little regard for Western medicine, and indeed entered a hospital just once, in 1973, to have his prostate removed. His illness set him back more mentally than physically. He lost some of his zest for life.

The summer day I surprised my father with an adopted two-month-old grandson he did not even know was coming, his spark returned. Though we were accustomed to letting ourselves in, we rang the bell. Before he could see what I was carrying, we asked him to call my mother, who asked only if she needed to put shoes on (which was code for "Do we have company?"). He said no. By the time she made her appearance, I had put Johnny in his grandfather's arms. He had enough vision left to distinguish that Johnny's eyes were almost the same hue as his own. The fact that we had given him Martin for a middle name brought tears to my father's still beautiful blue eyes. Beaming, he kept wanting reassurance that we would not have to give Johnny back. Before Johnny was two, I took him to Catskill for the first

Johnny, age four, playing with his Opa Martin.

time so I could bring back pictures of us together in my place of birth. He brought his *Opa* smooth river rocks from the Hudson and from New York City a miniature Statue of Liberty. Once more my father's eyes welled up with tears. For four years he made his "Little Man" laugh by nonsense-talking in German. As a loving *Opa* would, he sang to him, played with him, made clown faces at him, told him stories, and held his hand patiently and firmly whenever they walked together, as he had held mine, to keep him safe. My father often said that if it were possible to be reborn before dying, he had been reborn in Johnny.

When he was eighty-eight, my father's aorta ruptured late one night while my mother was fixing him some tea. He died before she got back to the bedroom. Neither of us got to say goodbye. It is not hard to understand why a force like my father believed in reincarnation; it is harder to imagine a world that he is not exploring somewhere still. If he is, it is easy to believe that once more he will find his way home to a river, and perhaps to another child, another daughter whose spirit his river feeds.

BAREFOOT IN THE CONCHOS

L U C I N A was the youngest and most beautiful girl in a family of twelve. She was the precocious one, the headstrong one, the brave one, the talented one, the one with a voice more beautiful than the mockingbird's song at dawn, the one whose hands danced on ivory keys, turned simple food into repasts, sprouted trees from seeds, laid bricks to build rooms, enwrought rainbows into ordinary cloth. She was my mother.

When my mother was born on February 2, 1910, in Camargo, Chihuahua, where the *Río Conchos* was its most impressive, times in Mexico were as turbulent as the river's headwaters. The Revolution hadn't quite taken hold but would within the year. Camargo became a hotbed of activity, with railroad tracks being pulled up or blown up, alternately, by at least two factions to prevent munitions from getting as far north as the capital of the state. Pancho Villa and his troops first took control of Camargo in December of that year. Jesús Lara Rey, my grandfather, decided that perhaps life on the border, beyond that turmoil, would be more peaceful. By then my grandmother Antonia had borne him six children, but two had died in early infancy, so they moved to the border with only four—Ofelia, Quintín, Toña, and my mother, Lucina. The peace that my grandfather sought for his family on the border was not to be had. The bloody three-day First Battle of Juárez in May 1911 sent thousands of refugees streaming out of Mexico and into El Paso. My mother came over the bridge in a trunk; her father determined that was the safest place for her. Many of those who came across the Rio Grande stayed. My grandfather, though, took his family back to Juárez. By my mother's account, he was an ambitious, hardworking produce merchant and property owner, but most of all a kind and loving father who showered her with attention throughout his lifetime.

If precociousness is an inherited trait, then my mother came by it naturally. My grandmother's favorite childhood game was to

Jesús Lara Rey and Antonia Lara Rey Mendoza, Lucy's maternal grandparents, with Ofelia (left) and Quinten (center), circa 1905.

dress in dirty tattered clothes and wander with playmates through neighborhoods away from hers, knock on doors, and ask pitifully if the mistress of the house had plates that needed licking. *"Señora, señora,"* she would implore, *"tengo mucha hambre. ¿No tiene por ahí platos que lamber?"* The game lasted until her father happened to be conducting business with the owner of a house she visited and heard his daughter's plaintive voice asking for food to satisfy her hunger. A razor-strop whipping ensured that she never played that game again.

My grandmother's childhood did not last long. At fourteen, she was called into the family parlor to decide whether she wanted to marry the young man who had come to ask for her hand; so nervous was she that she accidentally said yes instead of the no she intended. My grandmother soon became a mother. Young as she was, she had no tolerance for the mischief that her children, particularly my mother, invented.

My mother grew up in a household that lacked nothing. Wagons moved in and out of the neighborhood carrying produce to local businesses. The yard was populated with pigs and ducks and chickens and people to tend them. She and her neighborhood friends found the *corralón* a favorite playground, even though my grandmother forbade them to go there, for fear that the pigs in the yard would not take kindly to their presence. My mother found it amusing to swing chickens around her head to make them dizzy, then watch them stagger about trying to find their balance. I'm quite sure it was not fun for the poor chicken, a mite taxing on the heart. One chicken wobbled around for a bit and then keeled over dead. Coming out of the outhouse that day, my grandmother caught my mother red-handed and told her that she was to stay in the yard until she resuscitated the chicken. My grandmother put the chicken under a washtub and gave my mother a stick with which she was to beat on the top until she heard chicken noises coming from inside. The playmates left her to her mission. Her older sisters Toña and Ofelia were ordered by their mother to take turns making sure my mother didn't stop, instructions they complied with happily. She beat on that tub for hours. Dark descended on the yard, and still the chicken lay dismally inanimate. By then my mother was in tears, hungry and exhausted. Her sisters took turns having supper and returned to their task; my grandmother's discipline was relentless. My mother would have been there through the night if my grandfather hadn't come home and heard the drumbeat of the washtub and gone to investigate. He swooped her up and took her inside and proceeded to chastise my grandmother for so severely punishing his favorite child.

You'd think that kind of incident would have made a difference, but it didn't. There was a little girl on her street, Malena, who had very thick, very long, straight eyelashes. My mother called them *"pestañas de tejabán"* because they were like an overhang on a porch. For some reason, those eyelashes got on her nerves. She offered Malena several cans of pecans in return for letting her cut the eyelashes to a more stylish length. Malena was happy to sit still long enough for my mother to trim them, looking forward to the pecans. Indoors, the shorter eyelashes were no problem, but when she went outdoors she was temporarily blinded by the sun. Her parents were none too pleased, pecans or no pecans. Fortunately, Malena's eyelashes grew back. What punishment my grandmother imposed is lost to memory, but my mother always insisted that Malena looked much better with shorter eyelashes.

When it came time to go to school, teachers quickly discovered how talented my mother was. She was always singing, and beautifully, so my grandfather saw to it that she had piano and voice lessons. She was the one, he was certain, who would blossom the most splendidly, perhaps becoming an opera singer.

All the while my grandfather was also raising another family. The mother of his other children was Baptist and more cultured than my grandmother. She was the one who picked out the fabrics and patterns for the dresses that the seamstress made for my mother and her sisters. My mother and her siblings knew of their half-siblings' existence, but it was only my mother who accepted them and was kind to them when they ran into each other on the streets of Juárez. In my grandmother's Roman Catholic household, the word Protestant came to stand for everything that was indecent. My mother became a Baptist nonetheless; oddly enough, my grandmother was more accepting of her choice than were my aunts ever were.

By the time my grandfather died of a botched appendicitis operation at the hands of a drunken doctor, Antonia Lara Rey had borne him twelve children. The five survivors ranged in age from one in the womb to one aged nineteen. My mother was twelve. While the family was burying my grandfather, his brother—who had never approved of my grandmother—stripped the house of all that was valuable. The adobe houses that my grandfather had painstakingly built and was renting were all my grandmother had left to support her children. My mother continued with her schooling, finishing her *Educación Primaria Superior* at the age of fourteen in the *Colegio Bautista* in Chihuahua, a boarding school, thanks to an arrangement made before my grandfather's death. Even there, she got into trouble, coming in after curfew one night. No one would have known she was gone except for the fact that she spent some of the night perched in a fig bush and broke out in a rash. The teachers told her that the rash was *"un castigo de Dios,"* God's punishment for staying out late.

She returned to Juárez to help support the family and to ease my grandmother's housekeeping load. Young as she was, it was my mother who filled the long concrete corridor of the house with greenery of all sorts and planted the trumpet vine that would grow to form a blossom-covered roof for the twenty-foot-long patio. She filled the house with the sound of as many song-birds as were available at the *Mercado Cuauhtémoc*, but mostly mockingbirds, which she loved. To keep the birds singing, she gave them an occasional drop or two of tequila in their drinking water. She embroidered cup towels and tablecloths, crocheted and knitted blankets, and cooked. There was nothing my mother could not do well. Her talents and effervescent personality turned the house into a home once more.

At fourteen, my mother began her teaching career. Some of the students were older than she was. Her first classroom was filled with all the students who were somehow a problem to other teachers: some were slow learners, some were rowdy. They were nicknamed *"los gorilas."* According to her colleagues, my mother was a natural teacher who never had any problems in the classroom. She was disciplined, innovative, caring. Before long, all the rowdies—her *gorilas*—were walking her several miles to and from school and became very protective. Over the years, she took education courses, both in Juárez and Chihuahua at the *Escuela Normal*, to improve her teaching skills. Younger teachers coming out of a more modern university curriculum were sent to her for doses of practical advice for the classroom; she told one who was trying to teach about the earth's axis solely with dia-grams that the children would grasp the concept far better if he stuck a pencil in an orange. In 1939 she was chosen by her princi-pal, Srita. Otilia Rombach, to move with her and the rest of the best teachers in Juárez to the newly built *Centro Escolar Revolución*.

Raised on the site of the first school in Juárez, on top of a clandestine revolutionary-era cemetery, the school is an architec-tural masterpiece. The project, directed by Ing. Cesar S. Briosi, is of Streamline Moderne design, three stories high, with black marble staircases and banisters. Constructed over three years, in part by soldiers and jail inmates, its foundation is triply reinforced. Although it has suffered from lack of government funding to keep it maintained properly, the building has survived with no structural damage over the decades. All the inside doors are sectioned with glass panes; every room is flooded with natural light coming from outdoors. Its auditorium windows are leaded stained-glass images of Francisco I. Madero, Benito Juárez, Miguel Hidalgo, and Cuauhtémoc, the last Aztec ruler before the Cortés conquest—all revered Mexican historical figures. The auditorium seats the entire student body and has a full-size stage. In the school's sixty-five-year history, only three principals have headed it. All of the furniture is original, as are its slate blackboards; its murals are still intact, and on the second-floor walls are inscribed the names of all the teachers who opened the school, my mother's among them. Their picture hangs prominently in the principal's office. When President Lázaro Cárdenas came from Mexico City to inaugurate the school on March 18, 1939, he descended at the train station and walked several long blocks with the multitude who had come to greet him. Five hundred students a day still attend the school, and its teachers beam with pride at being part of the institution.

It was in that school that my mother spent her happiest, most fulfilling years. In rooms warmed in the winter with wood-burning stoves the teachers maintained, there were two shifts, morning and afternoon. She worked both. Each class had fifty to sixty students, sometimes two or three seated at desks intended for one. The facilities enabled my mother to cultivate her own talents as well as those of her students. The school had a well-equipped woodworking shop and a classroom filled with Singer sewing machines. In those rooms she taught boys and girls how to do both woodworking and sewing. In her own classroom, she

Group picture of teachers who inaugurated the
Centro Escolar Revolución, *1939. Lucina Lara Rey, Lucy's mother,*
is standing on the second row, third from the left.

taught them how to embroider, knit, and crochet. If her fourth-grade boys felt the necessity to fight about anything, she supplied them with boxing gloves, took them out to a sandlot, and refereed the bouts, making sure that they emerged friends. She also handled the unpleasant task of dousing occasional lice-infested heads of hair with the kerosene prescribed by school officials. Nicknamed *"petacas"* for her hippy defensive prowess, she played basketball with her colleagues as well as her students. With her beautiful soprano voice she was a regular soloist in the all-teacher choir—*El Orfeón*—directed by Edmundo Dieguez. Prof. Dieguez was so deeply enamored of her that he kept her picture next to his bedside, though no one knew of his love, not even my mother, until his family found the picture after his death. Out of respect for the fifteen-year difference in their ages, he never professed it.

Part of the two-month summer vacations was spent visiting family in Camargo, Chihuahua, her birthplace, where every year my mother would renew her acquaintance with the *Río Conchos*, wading in it and taking walks on its banks with friends. On the *Rancho de las Escobas*, the Ranch of the Brooms, she had a maternal aunt who conveniently scheduled her spring cleaning for when my mother and her sisters came to visit. The house had twenty-foot ceilings, and, like clockwork, when *las muchachas* arrived, she would be taking down the floor-to-ceiling curtains to be washed and ironed. While they were there, they also milked cows (part of the reason my mother never would drink milk), tended to other farm animals, and helped with the cooking. When they went horseback riding, they were told to be wary of the *chirrioneras,* snakes who hung from low branches on trees. At night, the ranch hands would encircle their beds with thick ropes to discourage the rattlers from making their way up to the mattress while the girls slept. However, for the better part of her time off she went traveling throughout Mexico with her fellow teachers, thanks to railroad passes and hotel lodging provided by the federal government. They regularly took the train to Mexico City, where they spent time in the floating gardens of Xochimilco enjoying the flowers, music, and food cooked on the boats. Guadalajara was another favorite spot. Even though she relished her vacation time, it was a joy to her to return to teaching. When she had summer suitors, they knew that come September 1, they would take a backseat to her students.

When the Lion's Club requested chaperons in the summer of 1946 for a charity dance to benefit the children of the city, she volunteered. This is how she told the story of that night at the *Plaza Alberto Balderas*, the downtown bullring. My mother went to the

*Lucy's mother, barefoot in the Río Conchos,
in Camargo, Chihuahua, her birthplace.*

dance accompanied by her niece, my Tía Ofelia's fourteen-year-old daughter, Graciela. Graciela took a liking to the drummer in the band. So to spend time with him more freely, she encouraged my mother to dance. Not that my mother needed encouraging. She loved to dance. Every once in a while, the band would do a song to which the men would go around in a circle in one direction, while the women walked in an inner circle facing them. The first time my mother spotted my father, it was from the back and her thought was "That's silly. Why would a sailor come to where there's no water?" On the second turn, she saw the blue eyes, those beautiful light blue eyes, and thought, "Hmmmm. Nice eyes. Hmmmm. Nice smile." The third turn did it. Their eyes met and he asked her to dance. The song was Cole Porter's "Begin the Beguine."

Into the wee hours of the night they tangoed to Carlos Gardel tunes, waltzed to Strauss melodies, polkaed to a *norteño* beat, and swayed to Glenn Miller songs. The evening was long on rhythm but short on talk, since neither could speak the other's language with any facility. Between dancing with my father and keeping an eye on Graciela, it was a Sunday to remember. When the musicians called it a night, she made sure her niece got home safely minus the drummer and went home herself to tell my grandmother about the evening. She announced that she had finally found the man she wanted to marry. Her mother's comment was something like, "Who would marry you? You're thirty-six years old!" My mother reassured her that this was the one. My grandmother wanted to know more. "Who is he?" "An American," she said. "What does he do?" "He's a sailor," she said. With that, my grandmother nearly busted her sides laughing. "Haven't you heard they have a girl in every port?" said she. "No. Not after tonight he won't. Not this one. This is the man I'm going to marry. I'll introduce you tomorrow." And off to bed my mother went, humming "Begin the Beguine."

On Monday evening she met him at the Oasis Restaurant next to the Plaza Theater in El Paso. He had invited her out for dinner, but not certain of the implications of accepting a full meal from the American sailor, she ordered a banana split. I'm not sure how satisfying their conversation was, but I guess gazing into each other's eyes was enough. He took her back home so he could meet her mother and made a good impression with his manners. The next night he came to get her and they went out again. By the third date, he had the engagement ring with him, one he had bought somewhere on his travels. Sounds fishy to me. Whether it was a sailor's tradition or his way of preparing for Madame Hahn's prophecy, he never did say. He asked her to marry him

Lucy's mother in 1946.

and wanted it to happen immediately. She said yes to the proposal, but no to an instant wedding.

So he got back on the train and went to New York, where he
signed up for another two years in the U.S. Merchant Marine.
From his travels he sent postcards and wrote faithfully, mostly in
English, other times in somewhat jumbled Spanish. He also sent
gifts from around the world—horn sculptures from Argentina, a
teapot and cups from Japan, a jacquard tablecloth from Spain
depicting the story of *El Cid*, and a mantilla for her to wear on
their wedding day. He sent jewelry from practically everywhere
he visited, including a more elaborate engagement ring from Civ-
itavecchia, Italy. There was a butterfly brooch made of mother-
of-pearl, a carved wood duck, and silver filigree flowers, jade and
pearls from Japan, red seed beads from Madagascar. When he'd
dock stateside, he would wire her flowers or chocolates. He never
knew that she had to pay duty on practically everything he sent.

In the spring of 1948 my father showed up in Juárez ready to
tie the knot. But my mother was not through with her school
year and would not have dreamed of leaving early. Endearing as it
was that her fourth-grade boys threw rocks at my father and his
car to discourage him from taking her away from them, she put a
stop to their practice. For the *Día de las Madres* celebration on
May 10, the boys sat with him as she gave her last solo performance at the school. She sang *"Estrellita,"* her favorite Manuel M.
Ponce tune. As is traditional for Mother's Day celebrations in
Mexican schools, there was folkloric dance, recited poetry, and
musical tributes. The wedding date was set for June 27, only a few
days after the end of the school year. She took very little time to
plan the event—less than a week—going downtown to Marcos
Flores, ascending the curved marble staircase of the city's best
department store, and taking whatever wedding dress was handy
that would go well with the Spanish lace mantilla that my father

had sent. The diadem that would hold it in place was made of wax to look like *flores de azahar*—the orange blossoms customary for Mexican brides; the Japanese pearl necklace would complement the gown. The invitations were ivory parchment to match the dress. The Easter lilies and carnations clustered casually by the florist were what happened to be available that day because she forgot to order them ahead of time. So busy was she with cooking the reception meal that when she was getting dressed she forgot the petticoat that went with the dress.

When she arrived at the *Primera Iglesia Bautista* a few blocks south of the bridge, she could scarcely make it up the long flight of steps through the throng. Those who had come to witness the ceremony, her colleagues from twenty-four years of teaching and her present and former students, lined the steps from the curb on *Avenida Juárez* to the church doors. Inside, it was standing room only. She was much beloved in the city of Juárez, as the person who wrote her wedding announcement proclaimed. Pastor Mateo Gurrola performed the ceremony, which included a long-winded sermon delivered while my parents knelt. I can just imagine my restless mother, wondering if she was going to get back to my grandmother's kitchen in time to save one of her dishes from burning. By the time she and my father got to the house from the photographer's studio, the house was packed with guests and my grandmother was looking forlorn, wondering if the food they had prepared was going to be enough. If they ran out, no one noticed, for there was music provided by some of her many friends and everyone danced into the night, my father making sure that all my mother's friends got to dance with him.

Oblivious to the fact that my mother had been working for days to prepare for the wedding, he was ready to leave when the guests did. My mother, too busy looking after her guests to stop and eat, was hungry. In her wedding dress still, she found an empty spot on the parlor floor, sat down with the dregs of a pot of beans she had cooked, and with a long wooden spoon scooped out what was left. She refused to go anywhere with my father until she cleaned up after the reception; he did not offer to help. Maybe all those years of restaurant work had made him allergic to dishwashing. He went to the Y in El Paso and came back three days later. It is hard not to wonder how my mother was able to sustain her commitment to their marriage when they were so different. He was the peaceful philosopher, content in his own world. She was a fiery mover and shaker, always wanting to make life better for us. They were individuals, with distinct personalities already shaped when they married. They began life together after each had lived a rich life; she was thirty-eight, he was fifty-seven. He was the love she had waited for by the river's bank. She was the love he had circled the world to find. Their unique union of separate, mature lives made them not only exceptional parents but interesting people. There were always "spaces in their togetherness," as Gibran would counsel. They stood together, "yet not too near together." They never stopped growing, but grew "not in each other's shadow."

My parents moved in with my grandmother while my father began the proceedings for my mother to become a permanent U.S. resident. My mother discovered quickly that my father did not let anything much fluster him. A leak in the roof over their bed prompted him to say that if she just moved closer to him, the drip wouldn't land on her head. If she was upset about anything, he would just look at her adoringly and say she was absolutely right. Whatever it was, she was absolutely right. Neither spoke much of the other's language. In their thirty years together, she spoke in Spanish to him and he spoke in English to her. How they communicated in the early years when she knew so little English is hard to fathom.

It wasn't long before my mother got pregnant. She did not know it when she went up Mount Cristo Rey with my Tía Ofelia and her daughter Graciela to pay a *manda* of my aunt's, a pledge made to God for a special blessing. My mother was known for wearing sensible shoes, but my fashion-conscious *tía* went in high heels, slipped about a fourth of the way up, and broke her leg. Graciela, who was about sixteen at the time, and my mother, had to carry my Tía Ofelia down from where she had fallen. The strain on my mother's system was too much and she miscarried. When Madame Hahn, the psychic in Shanghai, had told my father that the love of his life would be a dark-haired beauty, she also foretold this event and other of my mother's childbearing difficulties. My mother got pregnant again soon after. Her doctor told her she would have to stay in bed for the length of her pregnancy if she truly wanted the baby to live. My parents moved into Ofelia's house with her two children, Graciela and Sergio, who was then about eighteen. My mother had plenty of knitting, crocheting, and embroidery to keep her busy. She drew morning glories on a bedsheet and began to embroider what was to become a tablecloth. Her teacher friends made regular visits to keep her company.

When my father announced in early May of 1949 that it was time to go back to the Catskills, the pleas of my aunts and grandmother about the delicacy of my mother's condition did nothing to dissuade him. My mother never spoke about her own reaction. She dutifully packed their things, took her little black-and-white mutt to keep her company, and off they went. In the same car that had left them stranded in the Chihuahua Desert among the coyotes on their honeymoon, they set off on a cross-country trip. With all the car-related delays, it took them over three weeks. For my mother, the most memorable place for a breakdown was somewhere in Tennessee, right outside the fence of what was then called an insane asylum. The car had a flat tire and needed a patch, so my father took it off and went in search of a repair shop while my mother waited by the car. Men came to the fence to visit with her, one carrying a can of worms that he offered my mother for a snack. She pretended to take the worms in the same way that she would have pretended to feed cookies to some child's doll. Except for the fact that she couldn't communicate with words, the experience did not unnerve her. Among her summer responsibilities, she had regularly taken her younger brother to a similar place in Guadalajara for electroshock therapy purported to cure alcoholism. She was the only one in the family to brave the train ride with him, erratic as he was, and to witness the treatments.

I cannot imagine that she didn't harbor any resentment toward my father for taking her away from everything and everyone that she held dear. She had lived on the border in a vibrant culture all her life, surrounded by hundreds of people she knew. Suddenly she found herself in a country whose language she did not speak, in a dilapidated cabin in the woods without even basic amenities and no neighbors within miles. After years of freedom to go anywhere and do anything she wanted, there was nowhere she could go on her own. Her days were grueling. She cooked on a cast-iron wood-burning stove; to do the wash, she would walk down the hill to a stream that trickled off the Hudson River and then carry wet clothes up to the house to hang them out. The weekly pressing was done with a heavy iron heated on the stove. Her after-dark chores were done by the light of a kerosene lantern. The goat my father kept tethered to a tree eyed her regularly with sinister intentions. My father was gone to work most of the day, leaving her alone to heed the rangers' warnings of bears in the vicinity. She enjoyed the squirrels and the chipmunks, which were plentiful, but the chorus of katydids in the otherwise

silent woods took on too eerie a sound. To the sounds of the
katydids she added her quiet weeping for home on the border. In
letters to her closest friends she alluded to the hardships and lone-
liness, but mostly she told them of her day-to-day enjoyment of
the beauty that surrounded her.

With no hospital in Cairo, the nearest town to the cabin, her
doctor insisted that she check into Catskill Memorial Hospital
two weeks before the due date. Their car almost made it there,
stalling two blocks away. My father went on to the hospital by
foot and returned with a wheelchair. At the hospital, my father
signed my mother in, left her in the hands of the nurses and Dr.
Vincent Tuzio, and took off. I like to think that he checked on her
periodically, but he was not there when I arrived, a daughter, just
as Madame Hahn had predicted. Considering all the things that
could have gone wrong, it was a miracle nothing did; I was born
healthy about dawn on August 5, 1949, and was named Lucy (so
that the relatives on both sides of the ocean could pronounce my
name) Lara (my mother's maiden name) Fischer. My father so
loved the Mexican tradition of the mother's surname coming
last, that he would have preferred Fischer Lara. But they agreed it
might be confusing to people in New York, where they would be
settling. As it turned out, reversing the order would have been
fine. They did not stay long in the Catskills.

When it came time for the hospital to release my mother and
me, someone came to advise my parents to find a place in town
soon. The cabin was so remote and so ill suited for a baby
through the winter, the state might take me away from them and
put me in foster care. If my mother truly understood everything
that was said, I imagine her response was "like hell you will" or
"over my dead body."

When my Uncle Charlie came to the cabin soon after to meet
me, he took my mother aside and told her she needed to go

home to Juárez, that my father had been a bachelor far too long to know how to take care of a wife and child. He gave my father the money to send us back to the border. My father bought the ticket, drove us to the Albany airport, dropped us off at the curb with luggage and all those baby things mothers carry, and said "see you soon," or something like that.

Looking lost I'm sure, with more stuff than she could carry, my mother attracted the attention of an Italian family looking for the same plane as she. They asked her if she was Italian and she said yes, but was raised in Mexico. When she would tell the story later, she said it was the only time she ever denied her roots. The Italian family took her under their wing, and a young sailor joined the entourage of people helping her. This was the first time she had ever flown, and she was terrified: there was more than a little turbulence, and from her window seat on the wing, she could see an occasional flicker of flame. The pilot announced that although they were having a bit of trouble with one of the engines, there was no need for alarm. Before landing safely in Juárez, my mother thanked everyone who had helped her. She gave each of them one of the embroidered or crocheted pieces she had done while bedfast early in her pregnancy. Somewhere between Juárez and Mexico City, the plane crashed. There were no survivors. The Italian family and the sailor were among those who perished.

My mother and I lived with my grandmother in Juárez until my father arrived in his latest clunker, a truck that carried the furniture he'd brought from New York. He moved in with us, found work in El Paso, and soon found a house for us to move into, on Virginia Street, across from El Paso High School. My mother was relieved that it wasn't in the tenements right across the bridge. The house was a step up from the cabin, but having to wash diapers in the sink on a washboard was not much better than doing laundry in the Hudson. She decided that my Uncle Charlie was right, that my father was never going to be a thoughtful husband. Downtown at the Union Furniture store, my mother opened up an account in my father's name and bought herself a wringer washing machine made by Westinghouse. When it arrived, my father said, "The *husband* decides what he buys for his wife. *I'm* not going to pay for this because *I* didn't give you permission to buy it." Remembering that he was born in 1891 keeps me from thinking that he was an inconsiderate boor. She handed me to him and said, "Fine. You look after your daughter or find someone to take care of her and I'll go back to teaching and pay for my own washing machine. The washing machine stays." He must have done a double take, and asked where he was supposed to find a nanny for me. She told him that was his problem, not hers. After that incident, my mother became more and more independent. When they moved to the housing projects on Olive Street, the Westinghouse went too.

I started walking when I was nine months old and kept her hopping, especially with my early affinity for climbing, finding my way up to the counter and, one day while she was occupied in another room, nearly to the top of our short refrigerator. My father worked construction and was gone from early morning until late afternoon and for the evening meetings of the Building Laborers and Hodcarriers Union. My mother got pregnant again when I was about a year old. Alone in the house one night when she was four months along, she started hemorrhaging. Concerned more about my well-being than her own, she left a note for my father saying she wasn't feeling well and had gone to my Tía Ofelia's in Juárez. The driver got her across the border but then became alarmed as she grew paler and paler. Instead of taking her to her sister's, he stopped about where *Primera Iglesia Bautista* is on *Avenida Juárez* and told her to get out. He said she could skip the fare. She walked the remaining mile or more to her sister's in the dark winter, carrying me. My father found the note, cleaned up the blood he found in the house, and made it to Juárez past midnight. Ofelia told him not to worry, that she and her two children, Sergio and Graciela, in their late teens by then, would take care of us. Several days later my mother lapsed into unconsciousness and was near death. Holding her hands in his, my father prayed until she regained consciousness about the time that Dr. Valdez arrived. The doctor loaded the whole family in the ambulance because my mother was losing so much blood that immediate transfusions would be needed. It was her nephew Sergio's blood that saved her life, but she lost the baby. Yet another of Madame Hahn's predictions had come true.

My mother and I spent several months at my Tía's house while she recovered. My Tía became my *mama-otra,* my "other-mother." My first memories go back to our time in that house on *Calle Ocampo,* a few blocks from my grandmother's house. It had a hallway in the middle, with rooms going off to both sides, including a parlor with mahogany furniture and a big kitchen. Above the kitchen sink a window looked out into a backyard whose center was shaded by a huge mulberry tree. Sergio used to dance with me to the tune of his favorite mambos. As the music played at full blast, we sashayed in and out of the living room all through the house and outdoors. I was three when at a light on Paisano and St. Vrain, in El Paso, a drunk driver rear-ended the car Sergio was riding in. The impact sent him out the back door headfirst onto the median. Only twenty-one years old, he died on the way to the emergency room at the City-County Hospital. So fierce was my Tía Ofelia's denial that she refused to attend the funeral. Only when Sergio's body was exhumed months later did she accept his death. She never recovered from her grief. Until her death, many decades later, she dressed in black. I cannot hear the beat of a mambo without feeling the rhythm in Sergio's arms and seeing his smile. My mother's third miscarriage, that same year, was the last of Madame Hahn's foretellings to come to pass, ironic predictions given that Lucina was the Roman goddess of childbirth, she who brought children into the light.

Memories of my mother at the house on San Antonio Street all center around her building a home for us. Those efforts were visible in every corner of the house. Since my father had claimed the main room for his books, she worked around the barrister's oak bookcases to create a living room. It had a chimney, but no fireplace, so she built a faux one with a gas heater whose flames came up between ceramic logs. The bedroom the three of us shared was separated from the living room with a curtain. I remember vaguely having a bed in one corner of the room, but mostly I remember sleeping between them, even after my father had a nightmare in which he tried to strangle my mother, thinking she was a bully in a shipboard fight. When he was ill, which was very seldom, I was put on the living room couch. He had contracted malaria in the Pacific, and every once in a while he had a relapse and would develop high fevers that made him delirious. My mother allowed me in the room only to take him water or ice to bring the fevers down. His chills were so severe that the bed would rattle. During these episodes, I witnessed my mother using all her strength to hold him steady, giving him her body warmth. Bromo Quinine usually alleviated his fevers when he had these spells; he would not go to a doctor.

I was never far from my mother's side, and she was always busy doing something, always teaching me. I cooked with her, washed dishes with her, and after she turned the iron off, it was my task to iron my father's handkerchiefs with the remaining heat. As I got older, she would leave the iron on so I could do her hand-embroidered cup towels also. The towel assigned to Monday had a cat doing the wash in a tub with a washboard. Tuesday's had an ironing cat. When she sewed, it was my task to baste the darts on whatever she was making for me or herself, and then to press them so they would sit well as she attached them to the next piece. I was ten when I made my first dress. I also worked with her in the garden, where she tried to create beauty in the spots not cluttered with the junk my father was always bringing home.

When it came time for me to go to school, my mother enrolled me in the only kindergarten she would consider— *Escuela Primaria Agustín Melgar,* in front of the *Parque Borunda* in Juárez. To pay for my tuition, she taught fourth grade. To get there we took a bus downtown, boarded the trolley, then took another bus going east. She knew this would be the very best place for me to go to school. The principal, Srita. Luz, had taught with her before, as had her close friend Srita. Carolina, who had the reputation for being the toughest sixth-grade teacher in Juárez. Being the daughter of one of the teachers garnered me no special favors. I got away with nothing. There were far too many sets of eyes watching me at all times. The rules were very strict, stricter for me, or at least that's the way it seemed. One afternoon, I forgot that I was not supposed to cross the little pathway in front of the school and wandered to the other side to greet the principal as she was getting out of her car. She grabbed me by one ear, walked me across, took me into the office where teachers were waiting to start a meeting, and gave me a sound spanking. I learned my lesson. To add insult to injury, my mother repeated the punishment when I got home because I had embarrassed her in front of her colleagues. Talk about double jeopardy!

My mother glowed in the classroom as nowhere else. The walls in her room were covered with maps, multiplication tables, grammar rules, and student artwork. She taught poetry and arithmetic with the same passion. It was not unusual throughout her career to have fifty to sixty students in a class. The challenges she posed to her students were met with enthusiasm by both the children and their parents. When time came to plan celebrations for the school year, it was my mother who was called on. For *Día de los Niños* on April 30, she'd talk her fellow teachers into dressing up in outlandish costumes to sing and dance for the children. One year, in my father's cutaway and top hat, with fearsome makeup, she played the wolf in a musical production of *Caperucita Roja*, Little Red Riding Hood. Every grade had a significant contribution to *Día de las Madres*, Mother's Day, always on May 10. Within her classroom, both boys and girls did elaborate embroidery or hand-sewn projects for their mothers. Their recited poetry brought tears to the eyes of even those who professed to be unsentimental. Someone in the sixth grade always recited Guillermo Aguirre y Fierro's *"El Brindis del Bohemio,"* Mexico's most beloved tribute to mothers, which ends with a toast "to my mother, who in the darkest night is my star." *"A mi madre, Bohemios, que de mis negras noches es mi estrella."*

It was my mother's dream that I go to school in Juárez until I finished sixth grade. I made it only through the second before the authorities caught up with my mother and told her I must go to school in El Paso. She went back to being a full-time homemaker, seeing me off to attend second grade again because even though I could do the work of a third grader at Zavala School, she insisted that at seven I was too young to be in third. I came home at lunchtime to a hot meal and then walked the eight blocks back to school. Whether it was her lack of English that kept her from being involved in my school life or something else, she hardly ever went to my school activities. But she did all kinds of things with me and for me at home. For my solo singing debut, she made me an airy, sky blue chiffon dress with a silky azure duster.

Lucina Lara Fischer with her fourth-grade students at
Escuela Primaria Agustín Melgar, *1955*.

For my first play, *Twelve Bright Trumpets,* she made giant crepe paper daffodils for the stage. For a United Nations Day celebration for which I was the narrator, she helped me make my first dress in a sailor pattern with soutache braid on the collar and cuffs. Her masterpiece was a geometric designed, handpainted muslin dress that I wore for a play in the seventh grade. But my performances were seen only in her mind's eye.

When she wasn't busy doing projects with me, she was doing something to improve the house. For her most ambitious project, she first made a construction-paper model. It was to be a dining room with a room-length indoor planter and a wall of windows to let the sun in. After we collected rocks for a foundation, she ordered the concrete and supervised its pouring. She did more than supervise the spreading and smoothing of the twelve-by-ten-foot floor; she was right in the middle of it all, dressed in a housedress and short plastic rain boots, no gloves to protect her hands. My father was to do the brick column that would join the

room to the existing part of the house, but he insisted that it
didn't need any rebar reinforcement as my mother suggested,
and it collapsed in the middle of the night. Fortunately, an itinerant passerby looking for work had the skills she needed. She was
always doing that—hiring people that just happened to knock on
our door looking for work. They were usually fresh from having
crawled under or climbed over the fence that separated the
United States and Mexico, which we could see out our front door.
If it had not been for them, the house would have fallen down;
my father was of absolutely no use where repairs and mainte-
nance were concerned. He lived in his books.

When it came time to put in the Sheetrock ceiling, my job—
at the ripe old age of nine—was to hold up the T-shaped two-by-
fours to steady the sheet in place while my mother and her helper
nailed it on to the beams. For the rich ivory stuccoed walls she
wanted texture, so she had me run a broom vertically from the
ceiling to the floor. When she set the dark green vinyl tile on the
floor, my job was to heat the tiles on her electric griddle so that
they would be more pliable. She laid the brick rows for the
planter herself, and painted the bricks in another shade of green,
but did get help filling it with dirt. In it she planted aromatic Mexican jasmines, fuchsia-colored bougainvilleas, and flame-red
shrimp plants. She could grow anything from a cutting.

It was during the building of this dining room—her Green
Room—that she began to pass out. The first time it happened,
she collapsed in the backyard. Our dog, Blackie, licked her back
to consciousness, but she was too weak to get up. The insurance
man, who came by weekly to collect, found her and helped her
into the house, then went to get me from school. As time went
on, and the blackouts continued, she could sense the weakness
coming on and would try to make it to a chair, the couch, or the
bed. Sometimes she made it and sometimes she didn't, falling

hard wherever she was. I learned to lessen her injuries by lowering her to the floor or walking her to a soft surface before she
blacked out. When my father happened to be home during one
of her spells, he would sit silently beside her with her hand in
both of his until her color would start coming back. After what
seemed like an eternity, her eyes would slowly open and he
would put his hand on her forehead and stroke her hair. It was as
though he were concentrating all his life energy to bring her fully
back to life. Throughout the years, we explored the causes of the
spells with various specialists, ruling out everything from
epilepsy to a brain tumor, The diagnosis she trusted most was
that of Dr. Ramón Molinar Z., who told her that when she overdid it—worked too long and too hard—her blood pressure
dropped to the point that she lost consciousness.

Alongside those moments of tenderness were ones of great
conflict. While my father adored my mother, he wasn't at all
helpful in the side-by-side, day-to-day togetherness of making a
house a home. Once when she was struggling to dig a hole for a
rosebush, my father walked by and said he'd be right back. She
thought he was going to help. True to his word, he returned in a
few moments. "Darling," he said, "you're using the wrong shovel.
This is the one you need." And then he went back to his reading.
Leaks in the roof were of no concern to him. Every winter when
my mother would climb the rickety ladder to the flat roof to
shovel the snow off (with the right shovel, of course), he was
reading. Perhaps they had different priorities. Perhaps the difference in their ages or cultural backgrounds contributed to his
unwillingness to help. Perhaps he just didn't know how to be a
helpmeet. He left all the decisions to her, and all the work related
to the house to her also. He was notoriously bad—or good—
depending on your point of view, at bringing people home for a
meal without any notice. Usually they were people he met at the

Unitarian Church, interesting people as I recall, but it taxed my mother's energy to cook for more people on the spot. Many, many hours later when they left, he would retire to his room and leave the cleanup for her—and me. On at least two occasions I saw her take the dirty dishes and smash them on the sidewalk outside the dining room. I never knew who cleaned up the shards.

My mother watched every penny of the household allowance that he gave her. He expected it to serve for all the needs of the house; it did not. She always supplemented it with money from her rental property in Juárez that my grandmother had divided amongst all the children when they reached adulthood. He had such a love of learning and wanted so much for me to have what he felt I needed to do well in school that one day at a home show in the Coliseum he bought the latest *Encyclopedia Britannica*, which he intended to pay off bit by bit. Books he would go into debt for. Nothing else. They came before he told my mother what he had done. When the mystery box arrived and my mother opened it, she could not contain her anger. She carefully unpacked them, opened the front gate, then stood at the door and flung them out into the lawn one by one, in alphabetical order. When he came home from work, he brushed them off and put them in the bookcase. I'm sure I was the only child at Zavala School who had a set of encyclopedias at home, even if they were grass-stained and bent on the corners.

Whereas my father's routine involved bodybuilding and meditating, my mother's early mornings were spent in the garden. By the door were usually at least two pairs of her shoes, sopping wet. When she was watering and hosing herself off, she'd forget she had them on. To ward off colds, before she quit for the morning she would wet the uppermost part of her head, *la mollera*. After she came in from the garden, she would sit and play the piano, usually hymns for about an hour. She and I took piano lessons in Juárez for years from Srita. Dorita Chacón, who had taught with her many years before. Then my mother would work some more, perhaps start something cooking for lunch. At 10:00 a.m., with a cup of hot tea and a notebook, she sat watching Alan Ludden on *Password* for thirty minutes. She built up a tremendous English vocabulary watching Ludden and his guests, and spent time afterward looking up words she wasn't clear on. She filled dozens of notebooks with her word exercises. Even so, she was always hesitant to use her English.

Her routines did not change much throughout the time I lived at home. She taught occasionally in Juárez when called upon. After Zavala School, she sent me to Lydia Patterson Institute, a private Methodist high school in the *Segundo Barrio*. She was very strict; I was not allowed to date or go out in the evenings except for occasional school functions. When my piano lessons went by the wayside in favor of cheerleading, she was crushed. We had our share of mother-daughter conflicts when I was going through adolescence. My cheeks felt the sting of her anger on more than one occasion. I graduated from Lydia Patterson and went on to Texas Western College. Halfway through a teaching degree, an English professor twenty-five years my senior took a liking to me. It was the greatest test of my relationship with my mother. Having married a man nineteen years older gave her insight that I was unwilling to listen to as a sheltered girl of nineteen. Unable to contain her sorrow and so sure of the tragic consequences of my decision, she moved out of the house two weeks before I married. She went to Juárez to stay with my Tía Toña, who paid for my wedding dress from Marcos Flores, where my mother had bought hers, but didn't attend the wedding, feeling obliged to stay with my mother. At the wedding, my fifth-grade teacher, Mrs. Harrison, stood with my father, who never said one way or another how he felt about it.

In a month, she came back. Slowly the peace and friendship that had been ours was restored. In due time she came to love the man I married, partly because he spent weekend hours doing all the household repairs that my father never would. I used to tease her that if she had to choose between John and me, she would have kept John because he was so much handier.

A grandson five years later was an unexpected joy. After experiencing some of the same childbearing difficulties that my mother had, John and I applied to adopt but never told my parents. The difference in age between John and me was an issue for the agency. But then, on the morning of *Día de San Juan*, June 24, 1975, I got a call asking if we wanted a baby boy. I said yes and asked when. The voice on the other end said, "How does 1:30 this afternoon sound?" I spent the next few hours cleaning house while John followed me around reading aloud the section in the *Better Homes and Gardens Baby Book* that pertained to two-month-olds. We picked him up and on the spot named him after his paternal and maternal grandfathers, as is the tradition in John's Mississippi family. Johnny, John Martin West, came with the clothes on his back, two bottles of formula, a bar of soap, and no instructions.

We went to our favorite J. C. Penney store at Fox Plaza Shopping Center to get the basics so he would not have to sleep naked in a bureau drawer. By that time, the poor child needed changing. I had never changed a diaper in my life. My mother, who had given up hope of ever having a grandchild, volunteered for the duty but thought Johnny needed airing out first. He squirted her thoroughly and they bonded immediately. When we came home over the mountain at dusk after visiting John's relatives, the sky was on fire with streaks of reds and yellows. Opening the front door, we heard crickets chirp a welcome. Our good-omen crickets stayed through the summer and came back for many years after that. While Johnny was still a babe in arms, my mother taught him how to mambo. Anytime she babysat, I would find them both covered in mud or soaked from playing with the hose, their shoes by the backdoor. On St. John the Baptist's Day, to celebrate his becoming a part of the family, she doused him with water from the hose and he did the same to her. She sat front row, center, any time he was featured in piano recitals and went to all his plays. All the words she had learned watching *Password* on television finally got some use, for Johnny never learned to speak Spanish.

My mother took good care of my father until his death at eighty-eight. One week after he died, she asked me to come get all the books and bookcases he had left me. In their place she put plants and continued to fill her days with gardening and cooking and creating wonderful needlework projects. She lived alone, so her passing-out spells concerned me constantly. When she was

Lucy's mother with Johnny, age 4, 1979.

seventy-eight, we bought her a house two doors down from us so we could look after her. Before she left the one on San Antonio Street, she first uprooted all her bougainvilleas and jasmines in the planter in her Green Room, chopped them up, and put them in the garbage. Then she hauled out the dirt bucket by bucket, and finally took a sledgehammer to the planter and tossed the bricks over the back fence into the Franklin Canal, one by one.

It was only because she did not want me to worry about her that she agreed to move closer to us. She had taken the house my father bought without consulting her and spent thirty-six years on its preservation and improvement. I uprooted her; she uprooted her plants. Her frustration at growing old and not being able to take care of herself any longer had to manifest itself somehow. She stripped the extraordinary room, built with her own hands, and left it devoid of her special touches. Once she left, she never went back. The renter's checks came monthly by mail, and if there were any repairs to be done, John and I took care of them.

In the years that followed my father's death, we traveled together at every opportunity—San Diego, Santa Fe, San Antonio. When Johnny got old enough, she took us to Mexico City and Guadalajara. Whether it was a beach at San Diego or Puerto Vallarta, Lake Chapala in Jalisco, or streams in New Mexico, my mother was always taking her shoes off to let the water run over her feet. At the *Santuario de Chimayó*, she took a handful of the healing dirt and sprinkled it on her head, as I had seen her do with water every morning after she gardened, and afterward encouraged Johnny to befriend a beagle while she sat with her feet in the irrigation ditch. Even during her last spring, while visiting the San Antonio River, she found the perfect spot to go in barefoot.

Memorial Day Weekend of 1991, John, Johnny, and I took my mother with us to Chloride, New Mexico, to meet Shirley Watson, a marvelously independent friend of ours who was about my mother's age. Shirley drove us around all over and indulged my mother when she wanted to wade barefoot in a trickle of clear spring water off one of the back roads. My mother rolled up her pants above her knees and let the earth's pure water bless her feet one last time. Late that afternoon, she fainted on Shirley's porch. A nurse who lived across the street took her blood pressure, found it extremely low, and put my mother on oxygen. Johnny cradled her in the backseat and monitored her breathing while I drove us home through the Black Range Mountains in the brightness of a full moon. I was grateful for the moon's presence for I am a terrible night driver and the unfamiliar mountain road seemed narrower and more treacherous at every curve. Once we were home it took me two days to persuade her to seek medical attention. The doctor ordered tests, but, true to her lifetime of health-related enigmas, nothing conclusive was found. On another visit, Dr. Dwayne Aboud convinced her that she did need to be hospitalized, for her kidneys were beginning to fail. Dialysis left her weak, but when her nephrologist promised she could do it on an outpatient basis a bit of her sparkle returned. The night before she was to be released, just six weeks after our trip to New Mexico, she was flirting up a storm with her doctors. Before we could pick her up she lost consciousness, and I had to decide whether or not to have her connected to a respirator.

On the way out the door I grabbed the tape of Vivaldi's *Four Seasons* that she often played. To have connected her to any machine would have gone against the promises I had made to her. John, Johnny, and I held her and let the tape run until she drew her last breath and "Winter" came to an end. Over the following three days, Johnny folded one perfect origami crane for every year of his *mamacita*'s life. At her funeral, I played the tape once more, as loudly as the funeral home allowed, to celebrate the seasons of her life through which she sang and danced. On her flower-laden casket, Johnny placed the eighty-one cranes. All those attending who had been touched by her friendship took one in remembrance. The hot summer breeze took the rest.

GROWING UP ON BOTH SIDES
OF THE RIO GRANDE

IN THE YEARS before her marriage, my mother had been terrified of living on the north side of the Rio Grande. During her
early life on the border, her excursions north extended only as far
as downtown El Paso, especially to the Popular Dry Goods Store
where she shopped for shoes to fit her narrow feet and took knitting and crocheting lessons in English, though she did not speak
the language. To get to the Popular, she would walk up El Paso
Street, eyeing the tenements in the *Segundo Barrio*. She was convinced that all Mexicans who ventured across the border wound
up living in those tenements, a belief that then wasn't far from
the truth. About the time of my second birthday, we moved to
the *Barrio del Diablo*, where my father had purchased a small
house for $3,700 from a Mr. Brown. It sat in the middle of the 3300
block of San Antonio Street. Looking out the front door across
the empty lot, we could see the traffic on Paisano Avenue, the last
street before the chain-link fence that separated El Paso and
Juárez. Beyond that was the Chihuahuan Desert with its bounty
of *chamizos* and *nopales*. Behind us flowed the Franklin Canal.

Our block was one that in today's language would be called
culturally diverse. The Whites, who lived two doors down, and

the Thompsons, who lived across the street, were African American. The Greens—she Mexican, he African American—lived next door with their two girls, Patsy and Lizzie. My family's German-Mexican mix was unique to my block. The rest of the couples and their children on our street were Mexican. If for no other reason than the scant distances between our houses—a maximum of five feet on either side of some kind of fence—we all came to know one another. The boys in the house to the west found it amusing from time to time to use our chickens as targets for BB gun practice, so we maintained as much distance as possible under the circumstances. In his white and green-trimmed house across the street, Mr. Thompson, a jazz musician, used to play the piano in the early evening before he went out on gigs. Since the piano was directly inside the door, which was kept open much of the time, my mother would sit on the porch and tap her feet to his tunes. In the mornings he could sit on his porch and listen to my mother play hymns on our keyboard. Other than that, they mostly just waved at each other when they happened to be outdoors at the same time.

Mr. and Mrs. White were our dearest neighbors. Mr. White kept the most beautifully manicured lawn for several blocks on either side. When he wasn't working at the railyards, he was tending to their yard and frequently mowed our front lawn as well. When he did, he could count on my mother handing him a jar of her *jalapeño salsa*. Their backyard was home to a bounteous fig bush, and alongside the driveway were two tall silver locusts whose flickering leaves glimmered in the moonlight. Dressed in her crisp white nurse's uniform and cap, Mrs. White went to work early and came back midafternoon to complete her day inside the house. Early in the morning on Mondays, their wash-days, she and my mother would hang out clothes on their lines about the same time. On Sunday mornings Mrs. White, dressed in her finest with a hat to match, Bible in hand, would leave for Mount Zion Baptist Church about the same time my mother and I left for *Primera Iglesia Bautista Mexicana.*

It was fortunate for me that the Whites owned the house between us and them, and that they rented it to the Greens. Patsy and Lizzie and I spent many of our after-school hours and weekends together, mostly playing in my junk-laden backyard. My mother set up a wading pool for us against the Franklin Canal fence. The sound of the flowing water and the brush growing higher than the fence made it easy for us to imagine that we were out by a river somewhere. My father taught us how to turn somersaults on the A-frame sidebars of the swing set; to add color to our daydreams he gave me a beaten-up oil lamp that "might have been Aladdin's." In rubbing the lamp to call forth a genie who didn't always appear we wore off whatever silver-plating it might have had. The flat-tired old car in the yard became Cinderella's pumpkin coach. When we got bored with fairy-tale imaginings, we would take jagged-edged pieces of slate that my father had brought home and use them for our pretend school lessons.

Lucy at four in her backyard on East San Antonio Street, circa 1953.

There was always chalk with which to draw or write on them, and we took turns being the teacher. Sharing whatever roller skates we had, we skated up and down the front sidewalk, or jumped rope or played jacks or hopscotch. Under the watchful eyes of parents sitting on porches to escape the heat inside, we played in the summers till well past dark. By the time the Mouseketeers arrived on the scene in 1955, the Greens had acquired a television set. That evil box changed the neighborhood. It was Mickey Mouse who sent everyone scurrying inside the house at five in the afternoon. Sometimes no one came back out. The after-supper rhythms of jump-rope marathons, along with the summer evening squealing as we zigzagged in and out of the water arches that my mother teased us with, went silent.

Judging from the state of our houses, we must have all been about equally poor; practically every yard (the White's manicured lawn excepted) was part junkyard, part farmyard. Someone on the block had fighting cocks. As I've already related, my father brought home scraps of anything conceivably usable, and they mostly sat there, rotting or rusting, much to my mother's chagrin. We raised chickens and rabbits, and kept the customary Easter gift chicks and ducklings until they grew to become Sunday dinners. My mother managed our home with very little money, dividing her time between house and garden, always with a song on her lips. With little furniture in the house, we had lots of room to play. My father's books and mother's piano took up most of the front room.

Living that close to the border was an everyday adventure, and while the neighborhood had a reputation for being one of the worst in terms of gangs, I don't recall anyone voicing any sort of apprehension. If the teens who gathered under the corner streetlight every night were doing anything other than playing their instruments and singing, I certainly didn't know it. No one seemed to mind the steady stream of people coming across the border through holes in the chain-link fence to look for work. Only one time did I see my mother startled by a man hiding in our backyard. Using her sternest schoolteacher tone, she first scolded him, then fed him and put him to work. She fed countless strangers at our house, always at the table. These men repaid her kindness by helping her in the garden or by doing odd fix-it jobs around the house. The room she built onto the house with the aid of sporadic itinerant workers was her favorite room, the one where she sewed, embroidered, painted, and served Sunday dinners. Its table served many purposes.

My mother's insistence on schooling me in Juárez must have seemed odd to the neighbors. Some of the children on my block went to Zavala Elementary, others to Beall. The Greens were bused to Frederick Douglass Elementary School—this in the days before integration. It was my mother's wish that I do at least kindergarten through the sixth grade in Juárez; it was her intent to take me to school and just wait for me, but the principal talked her into teaching fourth grade. *Escuela Primaria Agustín Melgar* sat behind the *Escuela Secundaria* on *Avenida 16 de septiembre*, and in front of *El Parque Borunda*, then carpeted with grass and shaded by weeping willows. Every morning my mother and I would get on the No. 10 Paisano bus for downtown El Paso, where we would then catch the green, white, and yellow streetcar to go across the border. At *Avenida 16 de septiembre* we would get off and take the eastbound *Parque Borunda* bus to reach the school. The whole process took over two hours each way, each and every day. She felt that strongly about the value of the Mexican educational system she'd taught in for nearly a quarter of a century.

My time at *Escuela Agustín Melgar* was a wonder that I shall never cease to be grateful for. The first year there, I spent the morning in kindergarten and the afternoon sitting on the windowsill outside the first grade classroom while my mother completed her teaching day. When winter came, Srita. Luz Armendáriz, the principal, decided that I might as well go into first grade, since I already knew how to read.

We went to school ten months out of the year. Learning to print was not in the curriculum; we learned script using the Palmer Method. The classrooms were covered with maps to give us a solid foundation in geography, both Mexican and worldwide. We recited multiplication tables aloud, and the sounds of classroom voices wafted far into the park, which was kept green with well water connected to irrigation ditches. For reinforcing our scientific knowledge and spatial relationships, there were practical exercises in the park, like pacing off the approximate size of a

Lucy and her mother in their school clothes in front
of the Singer Sewing Machine store in Juárez.

Lucy reading aloud in first grade at
Escuela Primaria Agustín Melgar, *1955*.

whale. Taking that particular exercise a little too seriously, I walked backward into one of the wells and had to be fished out and stripped of my clothes. I spent an embarrassing day first wrapped in a towel and then in one of the teacher's smocks while my clothes were washed and dried. Our physical education took place under the weeping willows, where our activities chased away the grackles enjoying the park.

Music was a vital part of every day's activities, as was poetry. At the beginning of the year, the focus was patriotic, in preparation for *Las Fiestas Patrias* on Independence Day. I can still sing the Mexican National Anthem when the occasion calls for it. But the best times by far were the preparations for *Día de las Madres* on May 10. We were all part of the school choir that paid tribute to motherhood in song, and we were coached in the fine art of reciting heartfelt poetry complete with appropriate gestures. The following ode to a hanky comes to mind:

> *Pañuelito perfumado, que me dio mi mamacita,*
> *bien lavado y bien planchado, me lo pongo en mi bolsita.*
> *Cuando llora mi muñeca, cuando juego a la momita,*
> *yo saco my pañuelo, que me dio mi mamacita.*

> *Little hanky, perfumed hanky, that my mommie gave to me,*
> *Nicely washed and nicely pressed, I keep it in my pocket.*
> *When my little dolly cries, when I play like I'm a mummy,*
> *I take out my little hanky that my mommie gave to me.*

No mother went home without live flowers: red carnations for those whose mothers were still alive, white for those whose mothers had passed away. No mother went home without gluey, glittery gifts made by small hands, wrapped and decorated with Kleenex and pipe-cleaner carnations. No mother went home without echoes of melodies and poetry ringing in her ears. There was an abundance of pictures taken—not by parents, because cameras were scarce—but by street photographers who went from school to school capturing moments that would never come again.

I think my mother took great delight in keeping my existence hidden so that she could take me to school in Juárez. But my days at *Escuela Agustín Melgar* were numbered. El Paso school authorities didn't think too kindly of my mother transporting me across the border to get an education. The summer after second grade the powers that be insisted I go to Zavala Elementary School instead. Not surprisingly, since I was raised in a bilingual home—speaking English to my father, Spanish to my mother—and had two years of solid schooling by age seven, I could read and write

Lucy and her mother on Día de las Madres *at* Escuela Primaria Agustin Melgar. *1955.*

in both languages equally well, knew how to add, subtract, multiply, and divide. Warning me that I would be paddled for speaking Spanish in school, the principal at Zavala also tried to convince my mother that I should be in third grade. But my mother was adamant that I be in a classroom with children my own age, and so I went to second grade again, learning—very poorly—to print.

My second-grade teacher, who will remain anonymous, was unsympathetic to my restlessness born of boredom and my inquisitiveness about things not in her prescribed curriculum. Not knowing quite what to do with me, she made me her errand runner. That first year at Zavala, when we thought the Russians were coming after us, shrill bells signaling civil defense drills sent

us running for cover under the tables or to the school's basement—a far cry from the weeping willows and open sky I had
enjoyed in Juárez. During Rodeo Week, I remember looking
quite smart with my pin curls peeking out of my red cowgirl hat.
Since I didn't have the boots to go with the outfit, I didn't win any
of the rodeo tickets given out as prizes for the best dressed. The
white majorette boots with the tassel in front didn't get me anything the following year either.

The transition to schooling on this side of the border became
easier as I spent time with excellent teachers: Miss Ross, whose
library contained a wealth of resources to satisfy my curiosity
about a multitude of subjects; Mrs. Wiseman, whose strict discipline in math added to the skills learned across the border; Mrs.

*Lucy in her cowgirl outfit, ready to go to
Zavala School for Rodeo Days, 1956.*

Harrison, whom I loved so dearly that contact with her stretched over decades until her death; Mr. Yturralde, whose classroom was always bustling with creative activities, the most notable being a student-written and -produced play on the Spanish Conquest of the Aztec Empire. I was the narrator, decked out in long fake braids, an Indian headdress, and the muslin dress hand painted by my mother.

Throughout my time at Zavala, and beyond, there was Mrs. Josephine Nagel. She was tall and slender, wore glasses, and kept her long blonde hair pulled back in a bun. Almost year round, she wore a bright red hibiscus from her garden tucked behind an ear. Mrs. Nagel traveled through the school pushing a cart replete with sheet music, musical instruments, a portable record player, and an autoharp. At least two times a week we had music in the classroom, and after school twice a week there was choir rehearsal, preparing us for seasonal performances. Thanks to Mrs. Nagel, I performed in the cavernous Magoffin Auditorium at Texas Western College during a Trans-Pecos Teachers' Conference. From the uppermost center spot on the choir stand I gave confident voice to the cat's one *meow* in the "Brementown Musicians" song. It was Mrs. Nagel who took me back to the same auditorium to see a performance of *Tosca,* my first opera. It was she who introduced me to traditional American folk music, spirituals, and musical theater, as well as the European classics. Perhaps because music had played such a vital role in my Mexican schooling, Mrs. Nagel's dedication gave me a sense of security in a new environment while it enriched my knowledge of the universal language of music. I inherited part of her musical library when she retired from teaching, and for years and years, until she got too frail to get around, I could count on running into her at musical performances around town.

I would be remiss if I didn't relate a significant rite of passage from my years at Zavala Elementary—my first kiss. To protect his reputation, my suitor shall remain, like my second-grade teacher, anonymous. When we were both in seventh grade, he and I got to spend time after school together singing in the choir, he a tenor, I an alto. He was a little taller than me, dark haired, slender, and, as I recall, fun to be around. One day during a break in P.E., while we were sitting on the rock fence, he leaned over and kissed me solidly on the mouth, hard. I'm sure I blushed profusely because I can still remember my body temperature rising a few degrees. For several weeks he walked me home from school, held my hand, carried my books. Then his mother found out and forbade him to have any contact with me outside school. To add insult to injury, she even made him give back the kitten I had given him. The relationship was doomed from the start: I was Protestant; he was Catholic, an altar boy even, and very obedient. After the school year ended, I never saw him again. In all my years of living on the border, I have never run into him. I probably would not recognize him if I did. But one does not forget a first kiss.

Because my grandmother, *mi mamacita*, lived in Juárez, my connection to the city continued to be strong even after I stopped going to school there. At least once a week, my mother and I would take the bus downtown, then the streetcar to downtown Juárez, get on a bus going east to the *Colonia Bellavista*, then finally walk six or eight blocks to her home. Occasionally she would come to El Paso to spend a few days with us. Born in Aguascalientes in 1885, she was shorter than my mother. By the time I knew her, she had already developed a pronounced widow's hump. Her braided thinning white hair was twirled at the base of her neck, then secured with bobby pins. She put a little lime juice mixed with water on it to keep it in place, just like my mother did for my short, fine hair. Very rarely did she wear anything except a black dress. In her day, a woman remained in mourning for her husband until her dying day; occasionally *mi mamacita* would give in to my mother's insistence that she wear dresses in black-and-white prints that she had made for her. Most of the time she had on an apron in which she carried her orange and white pack of Faros. If something distracted her from a chore she'd started in one room, she'd walk off from a lighted cigarette and come back to a heap of ashes. Though her aprons were always scattered with little burnt spots and her fingers were tobacco stained, somehow she never set anything on fire. Her coffee, which she put in a blue-handled white enamelware cup decorated with multicolored flowers, was always cold, but she drank it anyway.

What I recall best about Saturdays helping *mamacita* is the constant activity on the street. The garbage truck, nearly as wide as the narrow street in front of her house, was the first to arrive. If we were there early enough, we'd see all the women haul out their garbage cans, wait while they were emptied, then carry them back inside. The postman's whistle called everyone out to get the mail. After that, there was a steady stream of street vendors. In my early childhood, the salesmen who didn't come on foot or home-engineered cycle conveyances came in horse- or mule-drawn wooden carts. Vegetables came in time to be cooked for the day's lunch. *Mamacita* had an icebox, not a refrigerator, so the iceman knew to knock on her door. Carts collected scrap metal, rags, splintered lumber. Men who sharpened scissors and knives came by regularly, pushing a pedal-driven grinding wheel. If we didn't want to cook that day, we would hail the man with the tamales in the galvanized bucket, the man whose slow, gravelly call urged us to buy his wife's cooking. In the afternoons, the *paleteros* rang the silver bells on the handles of their shiny white carts laden with Popsicles; young and old came out to indulge in one or two. *Paletas de limón,* made with the juice of tiny green limes and colored a greenish yellow were—still are—the best. Men carried huge packs of woolen blankets tied with ropes to keep them in bundles; others carried sample boxes of kitchenware and even small appliances. My mother knew these vendors and their wares well. The gold-and-green-edged glass dinnerware that matched our Green Room came from a street vendor. So did our blankets. My mother would sign a form for whatever she was buying, give a down payment, and the vendors knew to come back every Saturday for installments until she was done. They were agreements sealed with a handshake.

My mother had four rental houses in the same neighborhood, and every time anyone moved out of one of them she and I refurbished the place and readied it for the next tenant. We rescreened doors, puttied new panes of glass on windows, scrubbed and painted walls, and used muriatic acid on toilets not kept clean. Indoors, I learned how to patch walls with *yeso,* working nearly as quickly as my mother before the plaster of paris dried. All of her dwellings had indoor toilets, a rarity in the neighborhood. She made sure that the adobe walls were plastered as they should be, with mud and lime, not cement. Unlike other landlords in the vicinity, she did not hesitate to rent to people with children; her relationships with the people living in her houses were always cordial. It was not unusual for us to sit at their tables to share meals. Whereas her siblings refused to rent to mixed-race couples, or patronize a much sought after tailor who happened to be gay, my mother was never bound by the prejudices that plagued her siblings and always stood her ground for what was fair and humane.

My mother's and grandmother's speech was amply sprinkled with proverbs in the tradition of Sancho Panza. When I tried to do two things at once, they admonished *"No se puede chiflar y comer pinole."* (You can't eat *pinole* [finely ground toasted corn] and whistle at the same time.) If a dress my mother made fit perfectly on the first try, it was *"Te cayó como anillo al dedo."* (It fit like a ring.) And if a hand-me-down fit well, *"Tú tienes cuerpo de limosnera."* (You have the body of a ragamuffin—referring to the fact that a beggar would wear anything that remotely fit.) Of one of the Juárez neighbors who talked far too much, they said, *"Habla hasta con los codos."* (She speaks even with her elbows.) When I was going out to play, they would warn, *"No te vayas a meter en la boca del lobo."* (Don't go into the mouth of a wolf.) And to keep me from getting caught up in others' mischief, they sent me out with, *"Acuérdate que tanto peca el que mata la vaca, como el que le ata la pata."* (Equally sinful is he who ties the cow's feet as he who kills her.) Their proverbs can't help tripping off my tongue daily.

I also became well versed in folk medicine, because my mother, whether for lack of money or because she had more faith in traditional cures than modern ones, always tried home remedies first, both on me and on my father. A precocious and gregarious child, I sometimes attracted attention, and when I came down with an unexplained fever, she was sure it was *mal ojo*—evil eye. She proceeded accordingly, sweeping me with an egg and then breaking it into a bowl and putting it under the bed where I slept. Sure enough, an eye formed in the yolk, and my mother decided that a favorite cousin had praised me but not touched me, as is the Mexican custom. So she sought him out to break the curse by means of him passing three mouthfuls of water to me. Shortly after I was back to normal.

To reduce the chances of a sore throat, she would put warm saliva on her hands and spread it on my bare feet. If I still got a sore throat, it was lime juice combined with honey she poured down me. If I had gotten my feet wet, she made sure that I also moistened the top of my head to keep me from getting blisters on the roof of my mouth or catching cold. When I got sick and she didn't know what to do, she would call for my grandmother's wisdom. Once, when I was five, after several days of a fever that would not break, my grandmother took a handful of Snow Cap lard from the kitchen, stripped me, and rubbed me from head to toe with it. The fever broke as the chicken pox sprang. My grandmother's magical rubbing somehow made the bumps appear. Less dramatic cures in my house included *yerba buena* for stomach upsets, chamomile for calm sleep, cinnamon tea made with *canela entera* for a cough, oregano tea for a croupy cough. Aloe vera gel squeezed out from a leaf and spread on a wound served for most of my childhood injuries. A sliced wedge of garlic brought a splinter to the surface and drew out toxins left by thorns. Foul-tasting *epazote* sometimes soothed my menstrual cramps. Like my mother, and my grandmother before her, I use and trust *remedios caseros,* home remedies passed down to me.

When my mother couldn't cure me with *mamacita's* or her own remedies, there was a trip to downtown El Paso to Dr. Ramón Molinar Z. The office was at the top of a narrow flight of steps. The stairs were so steep and narrow that it was difficult for some people to get up them, and there was not enough room for two adults to climb side by side. The waiting room was nothing more than a wide hallway at the top, and sometimes there was no nurse or receptionist, not even a sign-in sheet. The doctor would just come out and say *"¿Quién sigue?"* and whoever was next would get up and follow him into the office. The barrister's bookcases held medical books; all the other medical-related furniture was white enameled metal. I suppose that made it easy to clean.

Tall, quite fearsome, very formal, Dr. Molinar Z. nearly always wore a three-piece suit with a pocket watch in the vest pocket. He had a bushy mustache and dark hair peppered with white, or maybe it was white hair peppered with dark. He had big, very strong hands and a no-nonsense approach to medicine. As good doctors can, he seemed to be able to tell from how I was carrying myself what was wrong. He would pick me up to put me on the examination table, pull out a tongue depressor, and most times declare that I needed a shot of penicillin, which he would administer. He made my mother promise that I would never get my tonsils out because that would ruin my immune system; I have them to this day. After I started school, I developed a very sensitive stomach that would act up when I didn't make perfect grades. He never made an issue out of it, said that if I were not an only child and had someone at home to fight with on a regular basis, I probably wouldn't even notice the less-than-perfect grades. I have the nervous stomach still.

Any place my mother and I needed or wanted to get to, we had to take public transportation. Quite naturally, our travels were limited by the bus and streetcar routes and schedules and the time we had available. It was about a two-block walk to the bus stop on Paisano Avenue and about a twenty-minute ride downtown. When we weren't in Juárez with *mamacita*, Saturdays were our downtown days. We would start by paying bills, stopping first at the Union Furniture store to give them a payment in person because my father didn't know she had opened up a charge account in his name. We would never have acquired furniture if it had been up to him. He didn't believe in credit, so she finally gave up waiting for him to save money to buy anything and just went down to the basement, filled out an application, and signed his name. She did the same thing at J. C. Penney, where she would get linens and things, as well as clothes when she didn't make them herself. She was a faithful bill payer, one who was never late with a payment and never, ever, paid interest on a credit card, paying the full amount owed every month. Our outings always included a stop at her favorite store, Grant's, where you could get everything imaginable, from clothes to kitchenware to pets.

The pet section was down a long set of wide steps. Our household menagerie always included a few goldfish and at least two canaries. My mission was to pick out the fish we would carry home in a cardboard Chinese takeout container. The canaries were a more studied endeavor. We'd stand for a while around the big cages and my mother would talk to the birds, whistle, sing, to see which one would respond to her. The canaries had to have personality or she would have nothing to do with them. If one cocked its head just so to the sound of her voice, it could pretty well depend on a pampered life in our house. After the choice was made, the salesgirl would put the fortunate bird in a bright orange box emblazoned with Hartz on the side and holes all around. Oh, how my mother would care for them—a cuttle bone clamped to the wire, a bird-seed bell suspended from the top of the cage, and of course one or more swings, depending on how tall the cage was. She even created custom-made covers to put over the cage when it was the birds' bedtime. The canaries lived in my mother's favorite space, the Green Room. When it was cage-cleaning day, she would let the birds exercise their wings and fly all over the house, and for the most part they would come back to the cage when she called them. There were a few free spirits who had no intention of returning willingly to the cage, no matter how gilded. Occasionally, the two of us, each armed with a kitchen towel, would have to pursue them, corner them, and toss a towel over their terrified little heads, then gently pick them up and soothe their ruffled feathers. We would hold them until their agitated hearts got back to normal after all the excitement and then deposit them in their clean cages. One passed out once, and my mother breathed into his tiny mouth to revive him.

She never liked parakeets, because they didn't sing. Since our house was always filled with music, the canaries added to the melodies—to the classics like Vivaldi's *Four Seasons* and to the Mexican songs that she sang regularly. Next to her singing, they especially liked the sound of bagpipe music sent by our Scottish friends, the Devlins.

In the days of food counters in stores, drugstores or otherwise, we had several to choose from in downtown El Paso. Newberry's was the closest to our bus stop to go home, so we generally had ice cream there before boarding the bus. S. H. Kress was the farthest, across from San Jacinto Plaza where we would visit with the alligators while we waited to connect to other buses, and from time to time we ate there. When I was barely able to handle a spoon, I so impressed the man sitting next to us with my manners that he gave my mother a dollar to get me a present. Grant's, though, was always her favorite place to eat, and generally that was where we would take a break or end our shopping excursions. She would order a breaded veal cutlet that would come with mashed potatoes and canned green beans or corn, and I'd get a quarter to go buy myself a hot dog in another part of the store and bring it back to the counter to eat with her. If she was not in the mood for the veal cutlet, which in time I came to love just as much as the hot dogs, she would get a bacon, lettuce, and tomato club sandwich with the little colored plastic swords in the quarters to keep them together. Our drawers had a wide assortment of plastic swords for when she made club sandwiches at home. Just up the street from Grant's was the Russell Stover chocolate shop. I guess the magic amount of spending money I was given at one time was a quarter, because I would go in and order a quarter's worth of Pecan Delights. I remember that there were more than two in the package. One I intended for my father, but sometimes there would be nibbles

taken out of it. He didn't seem to mind. Even when I had to
report that his entire Pecan Delight had disappeared on the way
home, he just broke into a big smile.

Special occasions called for new dresses, and my mother was
an excellent seamstress. Although she could make her own patterns and had all the tools with which to do so—a T square, a
curved ruler, tracing paper—we would sit together at *La Barata*,
or Grant's, and look through *Butterick, McCall's,* or *Simplicity* pattern books. Not until I became a teenager did we look at the
Vogue patterns; it was a rite of adolescence to look at the more
sophisticated fashions of the day. Of the half dozen fabric stores
downtown, I remember *La Barata* the best. There were two
floors, perhaps three, with bolts and bolts of fabrics for every
conceivable need. And taller-than-me circular racks of buttons,
cases with hem facings and corded bias tapes, pebble braid,
soutache braid, loop braid, and zigzag tape in a rainbow of colors. These were the packages that you could peruse at your
leisure. Behind a counter with a knowledgeable attendant was a
glassed-in case of laces and embroidered trims of every variety
imaginable, and ribbons to put in little girls' hair to match every
Easter dress ever made. When my mother was making her own
patterns, the saleslady asked all the pertinent questions: Was the
dress to be straight, princess style, ruffled? One piece or two? Was
the collar to be of a different fabric? What was the sleeve length?
Then she would raise her arms and flip a bolt of fabric to get
enough loose to measure me from shoulder to knee, take it to
the yardstick attached to the table, and give my mother an esti-
mate. They would visit a spell and come to a conclusion. They
always, always agreed that to make a truly fashionable full skirt
she would need three times my waist measurement to allow for
the best gathering. Before I grew hips, those full skirts showed off
my waist. Excepting a few ordinary dresses off the racks at J. C.

Penney, my clothes all the way through college were handmade by my mother, a ritual that began with shopping for everything needed in downtown El Paso.

A few blocks from downtown, three blocks from the bridge that crossed over into Juárez, on the corner of Fifth and Stanton Streets, was the *Primera Iglesia Bautista Mexicana*. Sundays were dedicated to church, and the tithe of my allowance was deposited religiously in the wooden, maroon felt-lined offering plate. Twenty-eight of the church's early members had been baptized in the Rio Grande in July 1892, half a mile up from the Santa Fe bridge; the church I grew up in was dedicated in July 1908. The $15,000 it cost to build had been raised by church members all the way down to the pennies collected by kindergarten Sunbeams. The church was white on the outside, and a wide flight of concrete steps went up to double doors that opened to a golden glow of oak hardwood floors and pews. The baptistry, with its River Jordan scene painted in oils, was framed in carved columns.

I was a toddler when my mother and I started attending church there. Bible in hand, I started the day with Sunday school. Then there was a long, long service, many times ending with multiple verses of "Just as I Am" sung as the minister urged people to come forth to accept salvation. My baptism by immersion at age eight was a major event in my life, made more memorable by the fact that I caught cold going from the basement to the sanctuary with sopping wet hair. I was a very serious child, zealous in my service to the church. Impromptu lunches at nearby cafeterias after morning services were followed by a trip home for a nap, then back to church for evening Training Union and another service. My occasional wriggling during an extra-long worship service was discouraged with sharp pinches on the arm or thigh from my mother. The usual Christmas pageants complete with wise men in their father's bathrobes and angels with wire-framed paper wings and precariously perched halos were rehearsed beginning in the fall and presented to a packed church. I wasn't a very graceful angel, I'm afraid. Hna. Reyes used to have a terrible time getting me to hold my hand just so, pointing gently up toward the Bethlehem star's stream of heavenly light descending on the earth. Playing the baby Jesus's mother was always out of the question for me since I was fairer skinned than the part called for and lacked the long locks Mary displayed in all the pictures posted in the Sunday school rooms. What I learned as a child in church was not wasted. Decades later at University Presbyterian Church, to give Johnny some of the experiences I had enjoyed, I directed *Three Wee Kings,* in which the animals told the Christmas story in song, Mary was a blue-eyed blonde, and the baby Jesus was a girl named April. After that came *The Best Christmas Pageant Ever,* where everybody wore their father's rattiest bathrobes, and Gladys Herdman, a most ungracious angel of the Lord, appeared to the shepherds and proclaimed "Shazam! Hey! Unto you a child is born!"

The *Primera Iglesia Bautista Mexicana* chapter of Girls' Auxiliary was directed by Olguita Reyes. GAs met on Monday evenings for Bible study and service projects. Imagine Girl Scouts earning merit badges for Bible- and missionary-themed activities. The steps in GAs went from *Doncella,* literally a kind of handmaiden, all the way up to Queen Regent-in-Service. Not only did we have to learn a multitude of verses—in Spanish of course—but we wrote essays, put on skits, helped with services, and volunteered to lead Vacation Bible School. My mother and I made hundreds of plaster of paris figures for the neighborhood children to embellish. If there was a task that needed extra pairs of willing hands, the GAs were there to help. On street corners we passed out literature to anyone who would take it, mostly in the *Segundo Barrio* where the church was located. We knocked on doors to invite people to come to our church. The only houses we did not approach were ones with prominently placed stickers proclaiming that they were Roman Catholic households and did not accept Protestant leaflets. We walked our little feet off carrying out the Great Commission.

For "Christmas in August" we gathered clothes and gifts to send to Baptist missionaries all over the world. Held in the basement, with food and costumes appropriate to where our offerings were to be sent, it was quite an event. Inspired by all the stories of brave men and women who lived in exotic places, some even with cannibals, I was convinced that I would follow in their footsteps. I was ready to be eaten by cannibals if that was what the Lord intended for me. I made it all the way to Queen Regent-in-Service, the top step, when I was a junior in high school. With a crown on my head, scepter in hand, and wearing a pure white satin pearl-beaded princess-style long dress, I was preceded by a flower girl strewing petals in my path and followed by a pillow-carrying page balancing the last emblem to be pinned on my green satin cape. To say that the ceremony was impressive would be an understatement. Each girl who reached Queen status had her own flower girl and page. We all looked absolutely angelic, a far cry from those girls who had smashed each other on the head with *cascarones,* confetti-filled eggs, every Easter Sunday on the steps of the church. From among us all, only Martha Peña has spent a lifetime in Baptist missionary service.

Schooldays were packed, Saturdays were spent either in downtown El Paso or at my grandmother's house in Juárez, and Sundays were dedicated to church; so only occasionally would we take in a movie. Never, ever on a Sunday, though, because that was on the list of transgressions not to be committed by devout Baptists. I was in college before I ever went to a movie without one or both of my parents, and each had different tastes

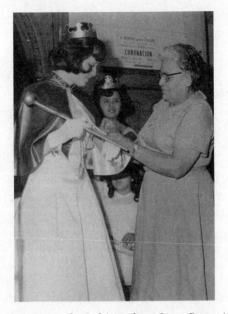

Lucy's mother pinning the Girls' Auxiliary Queen Regent-in-Service emblem on her at Primera Iglesia Bautista Mexicana *in El Paso, 1965.*

in movies they wanted to share with me. My father went for epics like *Spartacus,* classic Disney offerings like *Pollyanna,* and every circus movie that came to town. Downtown El Paso had an abundance of movie theaters, so we had many to choose from. The grandest was the Plaza Theater, with its red velvet seats from which to gaze up at the passing clouds and the twinkling stars on the ceiling. The State was a little lackluster, as I remember. The Capri had a Cinerama screen that seemed to put you right in the middle of the action; we all ducked when planes flew under the Golden Gate Bridge in a movie about the wonders of the modern world. The theater district extended south past downtown into the *Segundo Barrio.* It was to *El Teatro Colón* on South El Paso Street that my mother and I went most often.

When I first saw Disney's animated *Snow White,* it was dubbed in Spanish; I saw the film version of Hemingway's *Old Man and the Sea* in Spanish as well. That one became a special experience because Spencer Tracy and my father were built very much alike, from their full heads of hair down to their sturdy hands. Until my teens, I didn't know that *The Great Impostor*'s Tony Curtis could speak English. Movies with Jorge Negrete and Pedro Infante and Libertad Lamarque from Mexico's golden age of cinema sent my mother home singing the songs she loved so from her teaching days. I learned the fine art of satire, double entendres, and doublespeak from Cantinflas, the master comedian. María Félix played a *revolucionaria* with such earthy aplomb that when she sauntered into a saloon for a drink with the men, my mother spent a fair amount of time covering both my eyes and ears. No small feat. Between my activities at *Primera Iglesia Bautista Mexicana* and trips to *El Teatro Colón*, my Spanish language skills were considerably enhanced. I am most grateful for my mother's dedication to seeing that I never lost the richness of my Mexican roots, which began not with my schooling at *Escuela Agustín Melgar* but with her lullabies.

Besides the close bond with my *mamacita* in Juárez, the most important link to the Mexican side of the border in my upbringing was the ongoing contact with my mother's teaching community. Walking to or from the *Mercado Cuauhtémoc* beside the *Catedral de Guadalupe* to the *Mercado Juárez*, in a city whose population was then almost a quarter of a million people, we regularly encountered several of my mother's former colleagues, and the conversation would span decades. Most of them had taught longer than my mother's twenty-four years, some at the *Centro Escolar Revolución* where they had started their careers together. Rarely speaking to each other by telephone—most didn't have phones, or cars, on their very limited pensions—they came together on one another's birthdays.

They called these occasions *convivios*—from the Latin "to share life." Whoever had the birthday prepared whatever meals they could afford, got dressed to the nines, and waited. About sundown, teachers would start trickling in, bringing simple gifts and sometimes food and drink to add to the repast. Raul López would make fun of Otilia Rombach, his former principal, because all she ever had was *Pan Bimbo* sandwiches sparsely filled with meat; only ample amounts of beer would make them palatable, he said. Her specialty was *rompope con piquete*, spiked eggnog. Over the bare hardwood floor back and forth to her small kitchen Srita. Otilia would go, to wait on her guests. At Margarita Ibañez de Salgado's house there was always loud dance music and lots of food. She had been quite a tango dancer in her youth, and in her late fifties she still had a figure to brag about, especially in the bright dresses she loved to wear.

Most of these teachers were women. Some had married, but most had not, dedicating their lives to hundreds of children over the decades. When they got together, these women spoke not of their *achaques,* their maladies, but of how in their youth the Mexican government had treated them to free hotels in Mexico City and passes on the railroad from Juárez to anywhere the railroad went. My mother's favorite tale was of the regularly derailing trains in Chihuahua. *Las muchachas*—the girls—were so well known as a group that the engineer would send them to the nearest town on a handcar to bring back food for the passengers; if they were stuck somewhere for a night, no town, however small, lacked enough musicians to put together a dance in their honor. These women spoke of the thrill of teaching with a zeal that lasted their whole lives. They broke into song as easily as they broke into laughter.

By the time I was ten, it was understood that I would be baking the cakes for the occasions. How my mother and I transported sheet cakes across the border on the streetcar, I don't remember, but we did. On October 21 we'd take one to Srita. Otilia, whom everyone respected for her integrity as a principal; on November 4, it was for Srita. Carolina, whose specialty was scolding children and boxing ears, but whose garden was bountiful with violets with which she would make nosegays for her table. As they grew older and found it more difficult to get around, the crowd got smaller and smaller but no less lively. When I got old enough to drive, I would do the rounds in Juárez picking them up. One of the things my mother missed most about not living south of the river was the freedom to go anywhere she wanted on the bus, to see her friends, to minister to them as they got older. Many of them couldn't come to El Paso to sing my mother the traditional *"Las Mañanitas"* on the Feast of Candlemas Day, February 2, when her birthday came. Some had never acquired passports. There was one gathering that I especially remember. To the sounds of a 33 rpm record played on our Magnavox console bought at the Union Furniture store, Margarita led a conga line, weaving it in and out of the rooms in our house and then going outside, filling the winter night air with laughter and music. On the summer night my mother lay peacefully still at the age of eighty-one, those women who were still alive came to pay their last respects, gathered around her casket, and sang the melodies of their youth to wish her a joyous farewell.

When I go to Juárez now, following much the same shopping route as I did with my mother so long ago, I sing her praises for the rich cultural border background she bequeathed me. Outside the *Mercado Juárez*, I buy meat from a butcher who was her student, and inside I get spices, chilies, nuts, and vanilla from another, who reminds me every time I see him that Srita. Lucina was his favorite teacher. Traveling northward, I drive over the nearly buried streetcar rails on *Avenida Juárez*, passing the church where my parents married, and once over the border, I eye the tenements that are still there. *El Teatro Colón* is no longer a theater, but its marquee is a vivid reminder of afternoons spent there. Downtown doesn't bustle like it used to, and the Formica lunch counters have been replaced by charmless fast-food places. The house on San Antonio Street, long since sold, is nearly unrecognizable and no longer has my mother's well-kept garden around it. Mrs. White has moved across the street, but the silver locusts still stand tall in her old yard. Red-bricked Zavala School sits solidly, only now in the shadows of a concrete maze of roads, one connecting to the Bridge of the Americas going into Juárez. Time embellishes remembered images of my days in the *Barrio del Diablo*, of growing up with one foot on either bank of the Rio Grande. The memories flow as freely as did the river in its wildest days.

FOOD BETWEEN THE WATERS

WHATEVER TIME of day it was, whether you were walking, skipping, or roller-skating up and down my street in El Paso in the mid-1950s and 1960s, the aromas wafting out of most homes were unmistakably Mexican. Freshly rinsed rice hitting hot skillets sizzled; *comino*- and *cilantro*-seasoned *caldo de res* was a weekly staple; *menudo* with its dried oregano and freshly chopped onions was the Saturday or Sunday special; and when you smelled *caldo de pollo* you knew someone was sick. There was a *molino de nixtamal* within walking distance if you had a craving to make *gorditas* or your own *tortillas de maíz*. You got the *masa* to make tamales for Christmas from the same place. It was in my mother's kitchen in that small adobe home that I learned to cook. There that she passed down to me her knowledge of foods and herbs; there she fed my body and nurtured my soul.

The house I grew up in sits on a former riverbed. Paisano Avenue, the main thoroughfare to go downtown, and the site of the river's old channel, was the first street beyond ours, the last street before the fence separating El Paso from Juárez. The Rio Grande had changed courses several times over the years. Those occurrences flooded the poorest parts of the city, particularly the *Segundo Barrio*, and wreaked havoc with international boundaries. In time, a concrete channel contained the Rio Grande, and the Chamizal Treaty resolved the issue of where the border lay. A park with rolling hills of grass came to commemorate the peaceful settlement, but most of the time I lived in that house, the desert beyond the fence was our only vista. The Franklin Canal behind our house carried the river's water from the base of Mount Cristo Rey down the valley to feed the farmers' cotton and chili crops. The fertile riverbed we lived on explains why everything my mother planted grew. From the trees alongside the house she picked peaches, apricots, plums, and apples. All of these had sprouted from seeds or pits she had nonchalantly tossed out. Against the wall of the canal she built a raised bed to grow vegetables. What time she didn't spend on the garden, she spent inside, mostly in the kitchen because she loved to cook.

The kitchen was about eight feet square and on the east side of the house. Outside, between it and the chain-link fence, was just enough space to walk sideways, holding your breath. One day when I came home from school she was standing inside the sink, with chalk and yardstick in hand, marking out an outline on the wall where she intended to put a window. There would be nothing to see from this window save the neighbor's back screen door. Even so, my mother wanted light in the room where she spent so much time. The house may not have been very big, and it lacked many creature comforts, but it was solid, built in the early 1930s. Keeping her property in Juárez in rentable condition had taught her a lot about home repairs, but when it came to knocking a sizable hole in an outer wall, I had to wonder whether she really knew what she was doing. She did. She was never one to wait for things to be done for her, and she had the guts to attempt practically anything that needed doing around the house. After outlining the space, she got a chisel and a hammer and dug deeper and deeper, following the adobe lines. Someone with more strength would have probably taken a crowbar or sledgehammer and saved some time, but she knew what she was capable of. From time to time, she'd use a small pick, like miners use. As she took out chunks, she put them on the counter for me to carry out to the yard when I got home. Somewhere along the line, an itinerant worker happened by and she hired him to help her frame the hole with two-by-fours and put in a casement window. That is how there came to be light in our kitchen.

My father took no interest in home projects, but he was well used to my mother's. When he bought the house, its kitchen had no cabinets. My mother bought them, one at a time, from the Union Furniture store downtown. They were metal, plain white, and heavy. She chiseled into the adobe and secured a two-by-four at the height she wanted to hang them and did it, once again with whatever help happened by. Once they were securely hung, she and I took a long walk to the neighborhood Winn's about a mile-and-a-half away, where I got to pick out decals to dress them up. She let me place the decals wherever I thought they should go. Such a smart woman my mother was, in so many ways. I was invested in all her projects, so proud when we finished one, always looking forward to the next.

After she got through paying for the cabinets, she bought a kitchen table, red and gray, with a faux-marble Formica top and chrome frame all around. The matching red chairs had a marble design on their vinyl seats. That table and a freestanding cabinet were her work spaces. The purchase of the gas stove came next, one with an oven on top and storage on the bottom. That stove, kept painstakingly clean, was a source of pride for her. My mother knew exactly how it was put together, took it apart on a regular basis, and cleaned every bit of it until it shone. Eventually she replaced the sink, since she had put in a few dents and knocked out a few chips when she opened up the wall above it.

Resurrecting the tastes, sounds, sights, smells, and feel of my mother's kitchen doesn't take much effort. The small kitchen was devoid of many gadgets to help her cook, but her solid metal, heavy-ribbed, glass-container Oster blender got daily use. It whizzed through the fresh tomatoes and garlic that were the basis for so much of what she cooked. She chopped onions expertly and without tears, frequently singing or whistling as she worked. The memories of my mother's kitchen date back half a century and are a vivid, continuing source of pleasure for me. The aroma of the garlic, the sizzle of pureed tomato mixture hitting the hot cast-iron skillet in which she had browned her rice— these, happily, I can replicate in my own kitchen, whose drawers, I must confess, hold a gadget for every task imaginable.

Three times a day we sat down together for meals. Most of the time she didn't set the table but just casually flung the utensils on it. My father often said that if he ever opened up a restaurant, he would love for her to cook, but her waitressing skills left a lot to be desired. He was meticulous about his eating habits; my mother was just the opposite. She would scoop up food with her hot—often burnt crisp—tortillas and rarely use utensils except for soups. She rarely finished a meal without finding an excuse to lick her fingers.

My first recollection of cooking is of being lifted up onto a step stool by my mother so that I was waist high to the stove top. There sat a *comal,* a flat, round, cast-iron griddle with a handle, always ready to heat tortillas for at least two of the three meals. On days when she was not too harried, those tortillas did not come out of a plastic bag from the corner grocery store, but rather were hand-patted from lime-soaked, finely ground *nixtamal.* I would get a child-sized ball of *masa* to pat out my own less-than-perfect *tortillas de maíz*. Occasionally, my mother would use either a wooden or cast-aluminum tortilla press lined with wax paper to speed up the corn tortilla-making process. I had a smaller version of hers.

It goes without saying that our mainstay foods were Mexican. I've eaten corn tortillas since my four front teeth came together to bite into them. There is something ineffably elemental about the aroma of a freshly made *tortilla de maíz* browning on cast iron. That smell of the earth's corn cooking on the fiery hot metal evokes a treasured childhood in the kitchen working beside my mother. For her flour *tortillas*, she would use a red-handled rolling pin that she found at the old *Mercado Cuauhtémoc* across the border in Juárez. I had a child-sized rolling pin with which to turn my portion of flour dough into a lopsided *tortilla de harina*. Proudly I watched over our *tortillas*, mashing down both my mother's and mine when they puffed up. I developed a healthy respect for the hot *comal* on which I placed my creations, both corn and flour.

If there is another aroma that takes me instantly to the kitchen on the riverbed, it is pinto beans simmering in a clay pot. My mother's *olla de barro,* which I still have, has a reddish-brown glaze, with designs painted in cream and dark green. I wouldn't know how to cook beans in anything else. That John liked her *frijoles de la olla,* beans straight out of the pot, was probably one of the reasons that she came to like him as fast as she did, even though she objected strongly to our marriage. I never could understand why he would want to put salt pork or a chunk of bacon in the beans, except that it was a tradition in his Southern family. My mother's beans never had anything except a good amount of garlic and salt. They were a staple of our diet, along with Mexican rice garnished with canned carrot cubes and peas.

Not all of her dishes were so simple. On her stove, over an

open burner, my mother toasted *chiles verdes,* then wrapped them in a cool, moist cotton towel. At the table she would peel and de-seed them, then fill them with cheese or ground meat. With her bent-tined wooden-handled fork and a shallow bowl, she produced a rhythmic, musical clinking that turned two egg whites into a mountain of froth. After adding the egg yolks, she dipped the flour-dredged chilies in the fluffy eggs and fried them. In a process that seemed like magic to me, she transformed those skin-scorched wrinkled green chilies into plump, flavorful *chiles rellenos.* Her sauce was simple: garlic, sliced onion, and pureed, simmered fresh tomatoes, which she drizzled on top. Invariably, my fair-skinned German father would get the hottest one on the plate, and even though his ears would turn bright red and his forehead would break out in perspiration, he wouldn't trade his *chile relleno* for another that might be milder. Even today, my efforts with the wooden-handled fork are a dismal failure, the egg whites rising for an instant and then going limp in the bowl. Only in my mother's hand was that fork ever magic.

We crossed from one of the river's banks to the other to get the food to prepare in my mother's kitchen. It was a good thing that we lived in a neighborhood where the basics were available within walking distance, because my mother never learned to drive. But with her roots so strongly embedded in Juárez across the border, and my grandmother still in residence there, all the vegetables we used, and a lot of canned goods, beef, fish, and cheese, as well as herbs, medicinal and culinary, we brought across week after week. We carried groceries first in sturdy hand-woven dyed hemp bags and later, with the advent of plastic, in bright plaid mesh bags. The rituals connected with our finding the *materias primas* for food preparation were an adventure. It was a hunting and gathering expedition.

The walking required in our Saturday trips totaled at least

four miles. We started at the far end of downtown, at *the Mercado Cuauhtémoc* beside the *Misión de Guadalupe*, where we shopped for vegetables and herbs. The endless array of produce, sold by merchants of every age, was a palette of rich reds, varying yellows and oranges, and multiple shades of greens. The merchants' calls in the market were as colorful: *"Marchantita, marchantita, venga. Aquí tengo ricos tomates, aguacates, calabacitas. Ándele, pruebe este melón jugocito y dulcecito. Ándele, llévese estas tortillitas recién hechecitas."* It will lose something in translation, but it goes something like this: "Lady, Lady, here. I have delicious tomatoes, avocados, zucchini. Come, taste this juicy, sweet cantaloupe. Take some of these freshly patted tortillas." For cooking, she bought *hojas de laurel, orégano, canela entera,* and *cominos*—bay leaves, oregano, cinnamon, and cumin—a few kilograms at a time, in *alcatraces,* small squares of newspapers shaped into cones and folded at the top. We always got chamomile and spearmint to keep on hand for sleeplessness or stomachaches. And because my mother was as much a nurturer of the soul as the body, she bought an occasional jasmine plant, which she would carefully take out of the coffee can it was planted in with just enough soil to protect the roots, cradle it in a small plastic bag or a newspaper *alcatraz,* and tuck it carefully in her purse, or sometimes even her bosom, to smuggle across the border. These plants would flourish under her care, and the aroma of jasmine blossoms mingled with cooking food to fill our small house. After I started driving, she got more brazen with her smuggling. I thought for sure I was going to have my car confiscated when she bought a canary to bring home one summer. Right before we got to the inspection station, she tucked the paper bag under the seat. The claustrophobic bird poked through one of the airholes, got loose, and the next thing I knew, I felt his feathers on my feet. When the customs official asked what we were bringing across, I recited the litany—tomatoes, onions, cheese, bananas, papaya, avocados without the pits. I guess I must have looked honest, although I was terrified. Fortunately the bird had enough sense to sit still and not go flying into the inspector's face. My heart skipped a few beats during that escapade, and we never tried anything that bold again.

Our load from the *Mercado Cuauhtémoc* in hand, we trudged another three-quarters of a mile downhill to *La Florida*, a Chinese-owned grocery store and butcher shop where we bought beef. The store was a long corridor, with the butchers' area in the back. The area was small, with three chopping blocks and an ample supply of sharp knives in several sizes to cut through the quarters of beef hanging from well-worn hooks. Chava, the butcher, was quite fond of my mother. As a matter of fact, everyone she ever encountered on our shopping outings developed a fondness for her. Anyway, she would ask Chava for a *kilo* of this or that and he would raise an eyebrow ever so subtly to tell her whether or not she should stick to her order, suggesting other cuts that were fresher. Subtlety was called for, because from the end of the corridor, perched on a tall stool, the owner kept a watchful eye on all the goings-on. Whatever she bought in the way of canned goods and sugar was always rewarded with a *pilón,* a little something extra thrown in for regular customers. Another perk from the store owner was the yearly calendar at Epiphany, one with all the saints' days indicated, and illustrated with a scantily dressed Aztec maiden about to be sacrificed, or perhaps rescued, by a handsome, muscular warrior.

If we were out of cheese, it took another mile to get the only one she would use, at the *Mercado Juárez.* For *enchiladas* and *chiles rellenos,* we bought cheese made by the German Mennonite community near Casas Grandes, Chihuahua. For the sheer delicious pleasure of it, we bought *azaderos,* thin hand-swirled tortilla-shaped cheese, brought from Villa Ahumada, a small town 180 kilometers from Juárez. The *azaderos* from Villa Ahumada have a texture unlike any other and make mouth-watering *quesadillas*. Sometimes not all of them made it home. To give us energy for the return journey, we often slapped one on a fresh hot tortilla with a little salt we carried with us and part of a scooped-out avocado. Throughout my childhood, I do not remember ever getting anything in El Paso that we could purchase in Juárez. Beyond saving her money, the trips enabled my mother to immerse me in the world in which she had grown up and the culture she held so dear.

Once home, my mother would slice onions and toss them into a hot cast-iron skillet. While they browned, she would season thin slices of filet, which she cooked just long enough to leave them pink and juicy. Removing the meat and onions, she laid in fresh tortillas to soak up the juice. She called this dish *carne aventada*—tossed meat—and served it with some of the avocados and fresh jalapeño chilies we had bought at the market. It is still one of my favorite meals, although I don't alternate a bite of raw jalapeño with a bite of a beef-filled tortilla like she did.

The strong aroma of *caldo de pollo*—chicken soup—wafting out of any house on our block was a strong indicator that someone was sick. For her *caldo*, my mother boiled the chicken with garlic cloves, onion, and bay leaves, skimming it as necessary. When the chicken was tender, she added carrots, potatoes, zucchini, cabbage, and corn, usually in that order, the hardest vegetables first. Adding fresh cilantro at the end gave the *caldo de pollo* a little color and surely speeded up recovery. Smelling *caldo de pollo* coming from a neighbor's house was a signal to check to see who was ailing. Even on our limited income, my mother would bake something, then put it in a basket lined with a clean, well-ironed —usually hand-embroidered—cup towel and send me to deliver it while it was still warm. Sometimes she came along to see if she could offer any assistance to the family. Baskets, as well as pots and pans, circulated up and down our block, were never returned empty, and gave all the women who were lucky enough to stay home with their children ample opportunities to visit.

In our predominantly Roman Catholic neighborhood, you knew when it was Friday because households smelled of fish. And if you somehow missed seeing foreheads marked with crosses from Ash Wednesday, the forty days of mostly meatless foods left no doubt that it was the Lenten season. Even though our household was half Baptist and half Unitarian, the kitchen was all Mexican Roman Catholic. On the shopping trips to Juárez, we added a stop at the fish market, buying whole fishes when my mother's pocketbook allowed, or fish heads for soup when it did not. At either market we bought *chacales,* cracked corn to cook with onions, garlic, and *chile colorado,* and sprinkled with a little cheese; *lentejas*—lentils that my mother would turn into a very soupy soup and serve with chopped raw onions, fresh *cilantro*, and diced hard-boiled eggs; and *camarones secos*—dried shrimp—which she would combine with whipped eggs and a bit of flour to make *tortitas de camarón con tomate*—shrimp patties with tomato sauce. The Friday fish days were topped off with *capirotada,* Mexican bread pudding with as many variations as there are cooks. My mother's had *francecitos*—French rolls—toasted, then layered and drenched with *almíbar de piloncillo*—syrup made from dark brown sugar that came in solid cones and had to be wrapped in a towel and hit with a hammer to break it up before being melted over a low flame—each layer sprinkled with whatever nuts she had in the house, plus raisins, cheese, sometimes coconut, and topped with *grajeas*—colored sugar sprinkles for the final garnish. Seasoned with cinnamon and cloves, melding with the brown sugar and the other ingredients, *capirotada* baking in the oven was as much a treat to smell as it was to eat. For me, the Lenten season did not mean being deprived of meat, but rather being treated to foods not prepared the rest of the year.

Typically the word *tamalada* evokes the happy image of women who come together to share in the making of tamales for big family gatherings at either Christmas or New Year's. As the only child of a mother whose sisters did not like the kitchen, the *tamaladas* I remember were not gatherings filled with the raucous laughter and bustling but quiet, intensive collaborations with my mother. Instead of one joyous day of tasks split among many, it was two or three days of chores divided between just the two of us. It started with soaking the corn shucks and then cleaning them, which was my responsibility even when I was too small to reach the sink without a step stool. My mother cooked the pork, shredded it, and made the chili the day before the assembly; while it was cooking, she washed the pots that had grown dusty from lack of use since the year before, laundered the towels that she was to spread over the tamales to aid in the steaming process, and laid out all her utensils in the manner of a surgeon preparing for an operation.

The day before cooking day, usually several days before Christmas, we would either walk a mile or two to the neighborhood *molino de nixtamal* or take the bus downtown and at the same time shop for other groceries needed, mostly at the Canton Grocery Store, which would deliver whatever we bought. The *molino* downtown had a gleaming light blue chrome grinder. It was operated by a tiny woman, who even in her youth had difficulty transporting the buckets of lime-soaked corn from the back room to the grinder. She emptied the buckets, flipped the switch, and knelt at the end of the chute, waiting to test the coarseness and moisture of the *masa*. She would make any adjustments necessary, finish grinding, wrap the twenty or thirty pounds of *masa* in butcher paper, and send us on our way with a *pilón* of finely ground *masa* for making *champurrado,* a corn and chocolate hot drink seasoned with stick cinnamon and cloves that accompanied the meal.

Once home, we divided the *masa* into manageable piles, added Snow Cap lard, seasonings, and baking powder, then kneaded it and kneaded it until it was fluffy enough and light enough that a drop of *masa* plunked in a glass of water came floating to the top. With everything arranged efficiently, we would take a moist, clean corn shuck, spread a thin layer of masa on it, put a generous dollop of prepared meat in the center, fold the sides in toward the center, fold the tail in the opposite direction of the seam, and arrange the tamales around a cone in a dark blue speckled enamel canning pot. After filling the pot, my mother would cover the tamales with several clean towels and pour a liter of boiling water in the pot, just enough to steam them. In about an hour, the tamales were ready to eat; some were kept on hand for holiday visitors. Mr. and Mrs. White two doors down always got a dozen. After Johnny came into our family, he took part in all of the *tamal*-making rituals, including putting chili or *masa* on each other's noses when we spread it on the countless shucks. Whatever tamales didn't get eaten over the holidays were frozen for future meals. One of the hardest things to do after my mother died was to eat the Ziploc bag full of the last tamales she and Johnny and I had made together. Over the years that we all cooked together, Johnny developed a love for the kitchen, a fine-tuned sense of taste, and a respect for the rituals connected to our meal preparation.

Some of the day-to-day dishes my mother cooked were not what you would call epicurean cuisine, but it was all comfort food. For breakfast she often cooked oatmeal, and purposely let it stick to the pan to scorch for me. I have yet to find a pan that will

burn oatmeal (yes! truly burn—so delicious, as long as you don't
scrape too much off the bottom) to my satisfaction. When she
didn't do that, she made *huevos con tortillitas*—small squares of
tortilla fried until crisp, with an egg or two scrambled into it, seasoned with salsa. On Sundays we usually had bacon with Aunt
Jemima pancakes smothered in dark Karo syrup, or *huevos
rancheros* with mashed beans, or *huevos con chorizo*. When I came
home from school for lunch, we had *fideo, sopa de estrellitas,* or
some other kind of soup. For supper it was a piece of beef, pork,
chicken, or fish, and the two vegetables, one green, one yellow, as
prescribed by the food pyramid of the era. A lot of the vegetables
came from cans; after all, we could not carry enough on Saturday
to last the whole week. For variety she would sauté slivered
almonds in with the green beans, or throw in a scrambled egg.
She made elbow macaroni with ketchup or enhanced a couple of
cans of Campbell's Pork & Beans with sliced wieners; our bis-
cuits always popped out of cans. Her desserts consisted of Jell-O
with whatever kind of canned fruit she had in the pantry, using
their juice instead of water to make the gelatin. If she was too
busy to make dessert, Libby's canned fruit cocktail in a little
Pyrex bowl would suffice.

Two men infiltrated my mother's Mexican kitchen. One lived
in the house; the other one merely visited from time to time, ped-
dling his wares. My father was easily pleased with everything my
mother cooked, and although he loved her Mexican food, she
often tried her hand at some of the German dishes he liked.
There were always potatoes fixed in some manner or another for
him, usually to go with pork, his favorite meat. When she could
find pig's knuckles at the nearby Big 8, he considered it a delicacy,
particularly if she had the sauerkraut to go with them. Those
bones glistened when he got through with them, but he never
picked them up with his hands. Given a choice of sauces for his

mashed potatoes, he would pick not a gravy made from the drippings in the meat pot, but the same sautéed onion and fresh tomato sauce my mother fixed for the *chiles rellenos* that she cooked regularly. Up until the day he died, when my mother put a plate of food on the table before him, my father kissed her hands.

The other man was Morton Kolleeny. He worked for the Watkins Company, which has been in existence since 1868. In my child's eye I can still see him—tall with broad shoulders, possessing an abundance of dark brown hair, and wearing horn-rimmed glasses that set off his dark eyes. I cannot tell you how often he came to the neighborhood, but I do remember that not many people on the block encouraged him to visit regularly, either because the women in other kitchens were less adventurous than my mother or because money was more scarce than at our house. Like the rural peddler in a wagon laden with treasures, he came with a car full of everything a well-equipped pantry could ever hope for—spices, extracts, prepared mixes for lemon meringue pie and chocolate and banana puddings. And cookbooks.

In my mother's kitchen there were only two cookbooks: the *Watkins Cookbook* and the *Watkins Salad Book,* purchased, for $2.00 and $1.50 respectively, sometime in the late 1950s. Published in 1948 and 1946, and in my possession still, their pages are spotted and splattered, as all well-loved cookbooks should be. In those cookbooks she found ideas for all the potluck suppers we attended at *Primera Iglesia Bautista Mexicana.* My signature cookie is a variation of a recipe found in the *Watkins Cookbook.* To be historically accurate, it should be made with Watkins vanilla extract, which had a trial mark on the back of the bottle and indicated that if you were displeased with the flavor by the time you got it to that point of emptiness, Watkins would refund your money. Watkins still makes great vanilla, but they no longer adhere to their trial mark guarantee.

Morton Kolleeny's intrusion into my mother's Mexican kitchen was a mixed blessing. To be sure, it lent greater variety to her cooking, but her thrown-together meals were not only tastier than those with artificial flavors and ready-made mixes, they seemed to emanate from her hands in the same way my grandmother's meals and her grandmother's before hers did. Time spent in my mother's kitchen instilled in me a love for cooking. When I miss my mother most, I cook *huevos con tortillitas*. A fresh *azadero* melted between two fresh tortillas with a little *aguacate* on the side is a feast for my palate as well as my memory. I share meals, both simple and elaborate, with friends and strangers in my house, just as my mother did in our kitchen between the waters of the Rio Grande.

FRIENDS AND STRANGERS
ALONG THE RIVER CLYDE

MY CONNECTION to the River Clyde began five years before I was born. My parents had not yet met and the world was at war. My father was finally back at sea, in the U.S. Merchant Marine, his ship docked at the River Clyde's Tail of the Bank, at the river's deepest point. On June 6, 1944, D Day, while the troops were landing at Normandy, he was on a train traveling the twenty miles upriver from Greenock to Glasgow. The locals on the train included Elizabeth Mary Devlin, "Elma" for short; her mother, Agnes; and her Aunt Lily. Elma was a lively four-year-old. Attracted by my father's uniform, his outgoing nature, or both, she and my father became fast friends, even though Agnes was concerned that Elma was bothering him. Agnes was very shy, as was her sister; Elma's father Henry, a fireman, was out on a fire service boat, helping to watch their home shores.

Townspeople went about their lives, still numb with memories of the horrors of Hitler's ruthlessness. For two days, beginning shortly after midnight on the first Tuesday in May 1941, the Germans had blitzed Greenock and turned the port town into a vast cauldron in which 328 men, women, and children lost their lives, 626 were injured, and hundreds of homes were destroyed.

The glow from the searing blazes at the whisky distillery and the sugar refinery on Drumfrochar Road could be seen from Oban, a two-and-a-half-hour drive away.

From listening to the radio, and her father's singing, Elma had picked up the popular Jimmie Rogers tune "You Are My Sunshine," so when my father asked her to sing a song, that was the one she amused him with. He asked her where she had left her dolly, and Agnes replied that there had been no dolls in the shops since early in the war and that Elma had never had a "proper" doll. My father promised to send one when he got back to the States. Before leaving the area, he went to see Henry at the fire station and went home with him to spend the evening with the family, giving Elma a silver dollar as a keepsake of their meeting. The silver dollar is still in her jewelry box.

When he got back home, my father sent the biggest doll allowed by wartime parcel size restrictions. She was a golden-haired porcelain-faced doll dressed in a red-and-white gingham summer dress. Along with the doll was the biggest box of chocolates he could find, a fancy box with a wide red satin ribbon, a ribbon so treasured that Agnes dressed Elma in her finest dress, bobby-pinned the bow to her short hair, and had her portrait taken. That meeting on the train developed into a lifelong friendship, and he became Uncle Frank to Elma. Two years later, my father wrote to tell them he had met my mother and, when I came along, announced my birth. One letter that Elma kept offers condolences to Agnes when her mother died in 1952. He says, in part:

> I have learned to know that Death is but Birth to a higher
> Life. This knowledge has done much to assuage the grief I
> felt when my mother and father passed on. To know that
> they live in a better world and that we shall meet again some
> day, is a great comfort. All Spiritualist Churches have a mes-

Elma Devlin, age four, wearing the satin bow from the chocolates box sent her by Lucy's father, in Greenock, Scotland, 1944.

sage service where the departed souls can communicate with those they left behind. That so few people avail themselves of this service is mostly due to ignorance, superstition and prejudice. It is too good to be true. Most Churches are opposed to communication between the living and the "so called Dead" because that would lift Religion from the realm of superstition and uncertainty into the realm of science and truth. As for myself, I am not willing to accept anything that cannot be proved.

Then he shifts subjects to tell them, "Our little Lucy was three years old last Aug. 5 and is a big girl for her age." That's where the letter ends. Perhaps he ran out of time or paper. Or maybe he had said all that he wanted to say.

Letters and parcels with knots tied securely by Henry's expert hands came to our house every Christmas for decades, and for decades my parents sent packages their way. Usually they included something purchased south of the border in Juárez, and occasionally some of my mother's crocheted or embroidered handiwork. My father was the one who insisted on Emily Post-type thank-you notes for every gift bestowed on me, which I happily wrote. As my parents aged, I took a more active role in choosing the gifts and wrapping the packages. By the time I married, my father's eyesight was already failing—he was seventy-nine by then—and it fell to me to keep the friendship alive. Elma had married five years before.

It became my quest to someday meet Elma, Aunt Agnes, and Uncle Henry. Bit by bit, with sacrifices, the travel savings grew. When Johnny came along, Agnes made and sent him overalls; Johnny became the recipient of the brown-paper packages filled with Scottish treasures. Mind you, the Devlins never neglected the grown-ups in the family, but Johnny was especially spoiled— with toys, clothes, sweets, and books on Scottish history and lore. He learned as much from the books that Elma sent as I had learned from the ones Agnes and Henry had sent me when I was a child. By 1984, as Johnny's ninth birthday approached, there was enough in the travel fund to go overseas, not only to meet Elma, but also to see the last remaining German relatives, Uwe, Helga, and Birgit Buchsbaum.

I ordered travel information from the tourist bureaus of the countries we wanted to visit—England, Scotland, France, Germany, Austria, Spain, and Italy—and together we planned. The three of us each chose something in particular that we *had* to see or do. At the top of Johnny's list was Loch Ness, to see Nessie, of course, who couldn't possibly be a monster if it resembled the many images Auntie Elma had sent over the years. I wanted to meet my relatives in Hamburg, take a short trip down the Rhine River where we would spend the night at Oberwesel in a castle, then try to catch a glimpse of the hills near Salzburg that Julie Andrews had so magically brought to life on the big screen. We bought tickets for a special anniversary-year celebration of the Passion Play in Oberammergau, and I'd get to stand at the door-way at King Ludwig II's palace at Neuschwanstein and get my tonsils sunburned looking up at those magnificent spires. John wanted to see a bit of Spain and the plains of La Mancha. Johnny wanted to see the Leaning Tower of Pisa and the Eiffel Tower. That's what you get when you give a child books on architecture. From Johnny's book *Wings, Rails, and Sails* I had gotten it into my head that we would travel on every mode of transportation we could fit in. It wouldn't quite be *Around the World in 80 Days* in a hot air balloon, steam engines, rickshaws, and elephants, but what a trip this would be for a dirt-poor girl from a border *barrio*.

We would travel north by train from London to Aviemore; rent a car and stop at Loch Ness, binoculars in hand; drive along Loch Lomond and spend time in Greenock with the Devlins; make our way back south to Bristol and ultimately go across the English Channel by hovercraft; circuit Europe with Eurail passes; and spend the last few days in London. I learned so much by planning the trip that I considered becoming a travel agent. To secure lodging, I wrote to Oberwesel, to bed and breakfasts in six countries, and to one of Spain's *paradores* nearest Don Quixote country.

Coronado Travel Agency made what bookings I couldn't and sold me Travel Guard insurance. I found a house- and dog-sitter and recruited my mother's neighbors, Mr. and Mrs. White, to look in on her. I had not been away from my mother for any length of time since my father had died. I typed up our elaborate itinerary with as complete contact information as possible and made copies for several of my friends.

The Devlins were thrilled that we were coming, and Elma started planning her cooking and baking. In letters exchanged back and forth, Elma wanted to know what we liked to eat, whether we had anything special we wanted her to fix. The Buchsbaums looked forward to our visit as well, even though none of us knew how well we would be able to communicate. Only Birgit, who learned it in high school, spoke English. I'd learned not even a little German from my father. The rest of the monthlong trip was to be one beautiful sight after another, each city more full of wonder than the one before. There would be delicious food, lots of shopping, one experience after another to record in my newly purchased journal.

At our farewell stop at my mother's on the way to the airport, John helped her put a handle on a macramé purse she was making—and stabbed the palm of his hand with a screwdriver in the process. We left El Paso on June 2, 1984, bound for London and points beyond. The first stop was an overnight stay in Mesquite, Texas, to see our friends the Gibbens, who took one look at John's hand and saw to it that he got a tetanus shot before we continued on our long-awaited trip. We had an uneventful flight and arrived at Heathrow Airport on June 4th. I was so jet-lagged that I cannot remember any specifics of our first day in London, but Johnny remembers much and filled in the blanks for me: the initial ride on the Tube, wanting to stop and feed the birds at Trafalgar Square—and being told we would do it on the way back through—the bed and breakfast with the fish tank on the landing, the Jamaican housekeeper who astounded him with her "proper" English accent—different from anything he had heard in the South—being aghast that we would have to share a "water closet" with other guests, taking lots of pictures (which all turned out fuzzy) from the top of the moving double-decker bus on an afternoon tour, dinner at a Chinese restaurant, and going to the basement dining room to have his first poached egg, tea with milk, and broiled tomatoes—everything you'd expect at a full English breakfast.

Tuesday, June 5, we spent on a train headed for Aviemore, with Johnny suffering from the "are we there yet?" syndrome but otherwise content. We spent a lovely afternoon walking and exploring the shops there and then a restful night. On June 6 we put our luggage in a little red Ford Fiesta and were off, with John driving on what he called "the wrong side of the road" for the first time in his nearly fifty years behind a steering wheel. Nessie sighting was first on the agenda, but Nessie was elusive that day and we had to move on, first to Fort William for lunch, where we purchased a boy-sized bagpipe, then to Urquhart Castle, where we strolled on thick green rolling hills, climbed centuries-old steps, and felt the finest mists imaginable—as if we were inside a cloud. It was otherworldly.

A smooth ride along Loch Road and the banks of Loch Lomond was to take us to the Devlins. It was not quite dusk, and the light rain from Urquhart had followed us. To reassure the Devlins, who were putting the last touches on supper, we phoned that we were only fifty miles away. In front of us on the winding two-lane road was an elderly couple going the speed limit. Judging from the honking behind us, the speed limit was not the norm. The last thing I remember saying is that I didn't think we should pass them.

John pulled out anyway. He cleared the elderly couple's car, but then his brain tricked him. Instead of returning to our lane, he stayed in the lane he'd been driving in his whole life. Our little red sardine can of a car continued directly into the path of a bright yellow van. The major blow was to John's side. His right ankle shattered into many, many pieces and could not sustain his weight when he got out of the car to see about Johnny and me. Glass from his side window fell, gashing a third of his arm between wrist and elbow to such a depth that the bones were exposed. Even though I was securely strapped in with my seat belt and had braced myself for the crash with my hands, my forehead collided with the windshield and my jaw with the dashboard. The diamond on my engagement ring had been sheared off and my wedding ring was bent into my finger. The impact had shoved John's seat into the back, snapping Johnny's right femur in two and sending his leg up in the air. Blood streamed down his face from a slit in his forehead. Mangled metal encased him.

All these details I learned later from Chris Cleary, in whose arms I regained consciousness. Her son, whom John dubbed Red, was ministering to John as he leaned against a hog wire fence by the side of the road. Fortunately, the driver of the van, traveling alone, was not hurt. Moreover, he was a road-assistance driver, on duty. His yellow Automobile Association van carried a radio, on which he quickly called for help. Triply blessed were we because Red was a paramedic who knew how to keep John from bleeding to death. The magical castle mist had become for me a dark, disabling fog. I saw everything dimly but could do nothing. Men moved deliberately all around the car. Johnny was surely in shock; the only sounds I heard came from his rescuers and the Scottish equivalent of the Jaws of Life that they used to wrest him from the car. I was of no use to anyone.

It was forty years to the day from when my father had met Elma on the train. Supper grew cold at the Devlin's that night.

All of our luggage save my small carry-on was turned over to Chris when we were put in an ambulance, and she must have given me her phone number so I could reach her at some point. The closest hospital was at Vale of Leven, a tiny town. On the

way there, John was his usual self, cracking jokes with the para-
medics, causing one to note that "these Yanks never lose their
sense of humor." Another mentioned that it was the anniversary
of D Day. John's injured leg was thickly wrapped in some kind of
compression contraption. Johnny was on the other side of the
ambulance with his leg immobilized and having pressure applied
to his forehead to stop the bleeding. I was sitting on a stool in
between the two, trying to make sense of it all. I was not bleeding enough outwardly to merit much attention.

I'd not had much experience with hospital emergency rooms,
but was surprised to find that here there was no waiting in line,
no paperwork to be filled out before treatment. The emergency
room at Vale of Leven was well run, well lit, and not cold and
sterile. Although my ears had to attune themselves to all those
Scottish accents, the concern and sympathy of the staff there pen-
etrated my addled brain. X-rays confirmed my mother's early
observation that I was hardheaded to the core—the blow to my
head had not caused a concussion. By then I must have been
more or less coherent, because I remember answering questions
as I had glass pulled out of my forehead and chin and while the
inside of my lower lip and chin were sewn up. Some of my hair-
line disappeared under a razor to make room for what I jokingly
called strapping tape to close vertical slices on my forehead. My
sore jaws, body-length bruises, and sprained wrists were determined to be not of immediate concern.

John had been whisked away somewhere. I was left to hold
Johnny while they put eighteen stitches in his forehead; except for
the gash, his head had proved as hard as mine. Immobilizing his
broken leg as they settled him in for the night, the nurses told
Johnny all about the green grass and the rabbits and squirrels he
would see outside his window come daylight. Two policemen
were still there, offering assistance. I asked them to call the

Devlins in Greenock. The doctors who examined John came to tell me his injuries were too severe to be treated at Vale of Leven and that the following day we would be taken to Glasgow. Nonetheless, John was handling the incident quite well, wanting me to see to Johnny, who was indeed requiring much more of my attention.

I slept what remained of the night in a chair next to Johnny's bed. Together we watched the rabbits come to the window as the sun rose. At midmorning, two ambulances took us to Glasgow, thirty miles away, to the teaching hospitals there. One took John to Western Infirmary on Dunbarton Road. The other took Johnny and me up the hill to the Royal Hospital for Sick Children, where he was anesthetized and his leg set and put in traction. Once Johnny's leg was securely strung up, I walked alone down the thistle-lined road to see about John.

John's right ankle, suspended in a sling like Johnny's, had been pinned through the bone. His gashed right arm, immobilized to prevent scarring, was also suspended from a rail above the bed. He appeared to be in a torture device. It would be two weeks before his cut tendons could be repaired. Altogether, my traveling companions would hang in traction for five weeks.

I trekked back up the hill to the RHSC to Johnny's room to find a folding bed set up for me for the duration of his stay, thanks to a humane and caring medical system. By then, news of the American family injured on the Loch Road had made it all the way to a newspaper in Greece, where a friend from El Paso read it. But I had yet to call my mother. That would take more courage than I had in me that first day in Glasgow. Instead I called Gordon Bowie, our gruff and dour but caring Scottish minister back home. That phone call set in motion another part of the amazing support system that would see our family through this crisis.

Gordon had been raised in Clydebank, seven miles from downtown Glasgow. Clydebank had also suffered mightily during the war. In March 1941, it experienced a two-night bombing in which 1,200 people lost their lives, 12,000 houses were destroyed, and 35,000 residents were left homeless. Ironically, the bombs had largely missed their probable target, the shipyards where the *Queen Mary* and *Queen Elizabeth* had been built. Gordon's mother, Margaret, and his aunt and uncle, Jack and Beatrice Morrison, who had all survived that nightmare, lived there still. Before dark that night in June, there stood Jack in Johnny's room, dressed formally in a striped gray suit and tie, offering to be of any assistance he could. Jack, six feet tall and still strapping at sixty-seven, had a handshake whose strength was at once physical and spiritual. Johnny took to Jack's twinkling eyes and winning smile immediately. Jack became his Uncle Jack that first night.

Jack Morrison had an irrepressible sense of humor. Sweet and gentle Margaret and Beatrice, who came the next day, beseeched Jack with their eyes to cease his joshing and teasing, but it was exactly what we needed. I should have gained weight with all the chocolates Jack brought during the six weeks of John and Johnny's hospitalization, but the at least twice-daily treks between the two hospitals—1,300 steps each way along the River Clyde—and the lack of regular and familiar meals had something to do with a loss of fifteen or so pounds.

It was Jack who drove me the week after the accident to retrieve the luggage from Chris Cleary's—my first car ride since the wreck. As we whipped over those two-lane Scottish roads, I held tight to the armrest on the door and more than once flinched at the sound of sirens. I couldn't help it, though the last thing I wanted to do was make Jack think that I didn't trust his driving. Jack, true to form, was gracious enough not to notice.

Often Jack walked with me from one hospital to the other.

When the bruises on my legs were fresh, it was hard to keep up with his long stride and quick gait. Except when his secretarial responsibilities with the Hardgate Golf Club took him out of town, he visited both hospitals on a regular basis, sometimes with, sometimes without, Margaret and Beatrice.

Of all Jack's kindnesses, one stands above the rest. Just over a week after the wreck, when social workers noticing my lacerated and haggard face still stopped me to say there was help for battered women, when only the darkest tights concealed the black and blue on my legs and my clothes were already hanging loose, Jack invited me to Sunday high tea. That afternoon we walked from the hospital district around the green grassy knolls by the Museum at Kelvingrove and into Glasgow's very posh Grosvenor Hotel. If any sunshine glistened on the Clyde before that day, I had not noticed. My Glasgow had been cold and gray.

Jack had picked a perfect day for a long walk. We walked amid finely dressed and happy stragglers of a wedding party, and Jack introduced himself and me to them as they walked by. It was then that I decided that if Jack thought it was OK for me to be out in public even though I looked like a boxer who had lost her match, I would go out. Not long after, I began to explore downtown regularly.

It took the Devlins two days to catch up to us. Though Scottish police had gone to their house the night of our accident, we were already in Glasgow by the time the Devlins made it across the river to the Vale of Leven hospital. It was too late for them to go on to Glasgow that day, so they returned home. When they did catch up to us, Elma's arms were loaded down with baked goods, Henry's and Agnes's with books for John and art supplies for Johnny. The short visit that we had planned with the Devlins turned into weeks of camaraderie. Several times a week, after teaching music at Hillend Primary School, Elma would travel the same route by train from Greenock to Glasgow that she and my father had traveled decades before. I'd quip that her arms were getting longer from all the sacks of goodies she would bring. Her sesame cookies became my favorites. On Sundays the whole family would come, and Henry and John tried to outdo each other with their respective joke repertoires. Agnes would summon the smile of a wife who had heard the jokes before. Saturdays, however, became Elma's and my day out.

Elma proved a shopper par excellence. She knew where everything could be found at the best prices. So we shopped: for Liberty of London fabrics, for David Winter cottages, for St. Michael's lightweight cotton undies for Glasgow's cool weather. She took me to a kilt maker where I ordered a bright red Royal Stewart kilt with all the trappings for Johnny. He did not yet know his father's family were Sutherlands or he might have requested that tartan instead.

I lost so much weight that I had to shop for a new wardrobe. Elma kept an outfit I had made myself for the trip. We were like sisters too long apart—giggly, giddy, happy to be together. She made me neeps and tatties and cooked a haggis just for me. Yes, I know. Haggis for some is not a delicacy. But I enjoyed it then, and even still at Burns' Night suppers that come my way in far west Texas.

When I finally called my mother five days after the accident, I made sure my friend Ruth would drop in on her shortly after. Though she did not become hysterical, for which I was very grateful, she did not believe I was telling her the truth. She was convinced that John and Johnny had died in the wreck. Western Infirmary had a phone on a wheeled wooden cart available to patients. When I figured out how to pay for phone calls, John had it wheeled to his bed and he called her himself. There were two pay phones in the lobby of the Royal Hospital for Sick Children, several floors below Johnny. It was not until the end of the second week that I was able, with help from the nurses, to wheel him into an elevator and to the phone on which he reassured his *mamacita* that he was still around. Thanks to the extraordinary nursing staffs who would willingly move John and Johnny's beds, we managed to receive occasional calls from home at the nurses' stations. Ruth, who became my mother's support system, facilitated the arrangement on her end. Later Ruth told me that she had had strong forebodings as she drove us to the airport in El Paso but could not bring herself to dampen my excitement. When Gordon phoned her about the wreck, the news confirmed her feelings of dread. I made her promise to share all future premonitions, and she has been true to her vow.

Johnny remembers that it was not until the wreck that the trip got really interesting for him. He had a room to himself for most of the day and activities galore. The school year was still in session, and Mrs. Winifred Simpson was the orthopedic ward's teacher. She came by soon after we arrived and introduced herself more to Johnny than to me, telling him that she would be bringing by materials for him to study James I and II and the other British kings, so he wouldn't get behind in school. I'm not sure anyone had told her we were from Texas. She figured it out quickly though, even though Johnny has never spoken in anything resembling a Texas accent. After she left, Johnny was worried because he hadn't heard of any of these people and could not figure out what a monarchy was. Someone brought him a *Willy Wonka and the Chocolate Factory* audiotape, and he listened to it and a pipe and drum tape entitled *Amazing Grace* endlessly. He and I would spend afternoons drawing or coloring or reading, and at midafternoon the nurses would come by with a "picnic" of multicolored sweets. At 5:00 p.m. there was very British tea with milk and lots of sugar. He developed a passion for the Brits' famous brown sauce, which he put on everything. There was no television in the room, only one in the lounge, where he struck up a friendship with a beautiful little gypsy girl with the saddest eyes I have ever seen. In the distance he could see Glasgow University and the Museum at Kelvingrove. He wrote notes to his father at the Western, and John wrote back, as best he could with his left hand or with a great deal of effort using the hand suspended in traction. Karen Stewart, who became his favorite nurse, and Mr. Blockey, his orthopedic surgeon, looked after Johnny splendidly. (In Scotland, I learned, surgeons are titled "Mr.")

Down the hill at the Western, John spent his days in the men's orthopedic ward on the eighth floor, getting used to Scottish accents while off-color jokes were traded back and forth across the huge room; his companions were willing to tell them over and over until John understood them. Always the folklorist, John was pleased to add them to his collection. His arm served to teach young student nurses how to do proper dressings, and he got to where he could name all the exposed tendons. Whatever surgical procedures he needed were executed expertly by his surgeon, Mr. Waddell. The most frightening part of his hospital stay was the development of a blood clot in the lung, which was quickly treated with blood thinner.

When the sun set and darkness overtook me on my walks alone back and forth between the hospitals, sometimes the River Clyde became taunting. I wondered why I had ever wanted to come to Scotland. I cursed the childhood dreams of casting off from my Rio Grande to see other rivers. This river was anything but life-giving. When black clouds hung especially low and the icy rain was especially numbing, I imagined the Clyde swallowing me whole, sparing me from hospitals and pain and problems yet to solve. So focused was I on taking care of John and Johnny that I never had the energy or the time to shed tears.

As the days came and went the one thing I never worried about was the quality of medical care John and Johnny were receiving, and I was oh so grateful for the warmth and compassion with which it was given.

In some travel book I had read that if you ever found yourself in any difficulty in a foreign country, you should call the American embassy, or was it the consulate? At any rate, I got my coins together and poured them down the public phone in the lobby of the RHSC. I told my story to everyone up and down the bureaucratic line who would listen, but to no avail. No one knew what to do. I told my story to several airlines, who informed me that they could not transport us home under any circumstances. Finally I called Coronado Travel Agency back home. The agency contacted Travel Guard insurance, whose agents proceeded to make the necessary arrangements to get us back to El Paso.

Orthopedic surgeons Waddell and Blockey coordinated putting John and Johnny in casts on the same day in July. John's was a manageable knee-length, but Johnny's encased his entire right leg and was connected to a wide plaster band around the waist to prevent him from bending fully to a sitting position. It was reinforced with heavy nylon-threaded tape—a childproof cast, they said. John could not maneuver crutches because of his arm injury; Johnny, despite the constraints of his cast, could. I did not want to take them home without showing them some of Glasgow, and both doctors encouraged me to take them out on day trips, allowing me to use the scarce hospital wheelchairs when they were available until Johnny felt secure on crutches. Even the wheelchair did not make things easy. Because the plaster waistband kept Johnny from bending into actual sitting position, we had to, more or less, prop him against the wheelchair. Only the end of the footrest kept him from slipping out.

I suppose it would have been worth a try to wheel Johnny

down to the Museum at Kelvingrove and other sites within walking distance, but I had visions of catastrophe on the steep incline and doubted my stamina for the trip back up. I opted for a big black taxicab. I could hold the wheelchair steady by the bar across the top and help him scoot to the edge of the floorboard. Then I would cup my hands under the cast at the ankle and push him into the floor of the cab, boosting him once more so he could recline across a seat. I discovered how much a hefty nine-year-old boy weighs in a cast—and how much space he occupies. There was no room left for the nonfolding wheelchair, which I then had to return to the nurses' station several floors up while Johnny waited in the car. Nurse Stewart and her small car made possible a night out at an Italian restaurant, but putting Johnny in the backseat was an adventure. Getting him out was even more interesting. We joked it was a pity we couldn't strap him on top. At

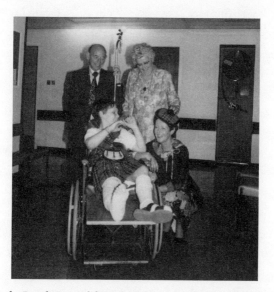

Johnny at the Royal Hospital for Sick Children in Glasgow with Elma Devlin beside him, Henry and Agnes Devlin standing behind, July 1984.

the restaurant, he ate reclined across two wooden chairs. I sat next to him in a third chair, his foot braced against my thigh so that he wouldn't slide off.

Elma cheerfully pushed John's wheelchair through the Botanical Gardens but lacked the depth perception to keep from running his cast into walls as she maneuvered narrow stone paths. At the Royal Fusiliers Museum, where we all went, the curator took a Glengarry off a statue and put it on Johnny's head; it had been donated to the museum by a man who had worn it in battle. At the Museum at Kelvingrove, the staff rode him up and down in their wood-paneled service elevator, the giant one used to transport sculptures to the various exhibit halls, and the concert organist played his requests on the mammoth nineteenth-century pipe organ. He felt the mocking of the magnificently carved flights of stairs that were inaccessible to him, but everywhere we went supreme efforts were made by the museum staff to give him the best experiences possible. They helped him create memories of Scotland well beyond the trauma of the wreck. The only piece of art that he never got to see up close was the original of Dalí's crucified Christ looking down on the world—a print of which hung in Gordon Bowie's pastoral office in El Paso.

We saved Glasgow's Burrell Collection for the last to let John build up enough strength to go. It still took two taxis to get us there; we brought one wheelchair with us, and I made arrangements to have a second wheelchair there. Once more we pressed Elma into service. The collection, housed in a modern structure, was fairly handicapped accessible. The museum itself was magnificent, built in the woods, with stained glass catching the sunlight that flickers through the leafy trees outside. The impressive Grecian urn dwarfed us all; every doorway had come from centuries-old structures, and every room held countless relics to admire.

When the taxis came to collect us, Johnny stood on crutches by the doorway while I put John into the first cab. As Johnny waited, the temptation of trees and grass became too great, and he went to take a closer look by the walkway. Out of the corner of my eye, I saw Johnny fall face first into the grass—like a mummy in a budget horror movie. His crutches went flying. A frail, very properly dressed lady, just getting off a tour bus, reached to help Johnny up, but slipped and landed on top of him. The vision of another six-week hospital stay—and the not-so-motherly thought of leaving him at the RHSC while I took myself on an extended vacation—flashed before me. But the childproof cast proved as strong as Mr. Blockey had said it would be. Johnny was fine. Except that he was laughing so hard in his turtlelike helplessness that it was difficult to turn him over, much less get him upright, especially since the white-haired Good Samaritan kept sliding back onto him. It was a scene worthy of Peter Sellers. Save for grass stains on her skirt, and her good-natured embarrassment, Johnny's would-be rescuer seemed to suffer no noticeable damage. That outing ended our museum day trips.

When the doctors granted permission for a Saturday night out on the town, the Mitchell Theater made last-minute accommodations for two wheelchairs, and we became the unwitting guests of honor for a Scottish Night performance of the Bobby Harvey Band, complete with the ceremonious piping in of the haggis. They bade us farewell with a solemn and most fitting pipe and drum rendition of "Amazing Grace." Johnny's nurses didn't even bat an eye when we wheeled in after midnight. The next morning we sat in humble gratitude in the gray gothic splendor of Glasgow Cathedral amid a congregation dressed in their finest kilts.

Travel Guard was good to us. They paid hospital bills and figured out how to get us home. They flew in Dr. Cohen from London to oversee the whole production. We were elevated onto the plane in a food service truck, Johnny still in a hospital bed. All decked out in his Royal Stewart kilt in the middle of July, he flew over the Atlantic lying over six seats in the rear, discreetly half concealed with a curtain and tenderly cared for by British Caledonia flight attendants. John had three seats to stretch out in, the doctor two, and I one. In Dallas, we were put on a Lear jet because no commercial airline would take us. On landing, Dr. Cohen took John and Johnny to a local hospital for observation. This time they had to wait their turn in the hall for several hours before they were taken care of. Gordon took me home, unloaded the luggage—wondering how I had managed to buy so much heavy stuff—and hooked up the air conditioner for me. That, more or less, ended the saga of the wreck. Shattered bones healed more quickly and thoroughly than shattered dreams. We never made it to Germany. It was eight years before we traveled out of the country again, this time with someone else at the wheel. We have yet to return to Scotland.

However, the time that Elma and I spent together cemented a friendship that is ongoing. We trade brown-paper packages for special occasions and speak regularly by phone—trading jokes, quipping about our disappearing waistlines, and wishing she could come to Texas. When she takes the train trip from Greenock to Glasgow, she is reminded of my father's first trip there; by the River Clyde she remembers how we walked together through the first major crisis of my adult life.

Travel Guard also reimbursed us for the part of our trip that we never used—the Eurail passes and the castle lodging. And so there was $3,500 "left" from our dream trip. Call it superstition if you will, but I could not put those dollars back in the travel fund. Perhaps I thought they would taint other trips. Instead, I built something: I added walls and windows to a porch with the help of two men, as I had learned to do from my mother. That room's centerpiece is a round oak pedestal table, over a hundred years old, which traveled from New York to El Paso when my father moved to Texas. On the wall is a mirror he took in trade for the price of passage home from America for a homesick Scottish girl he scarcely knew in the 1920s. In one corner is a Victrola, another keepsake from my father's years in New York City. Against the window is the sewing machine on which my mother made my dresses and taught me to sew. The china cabinet is filled with David Winter cottages bought in Glasgow on my Saturday excursions with Elma. I still hope to visit the lush green Scottish countrysides I have seen only in the calendars she sends yearly.

On the walls hang pictures from trips taken since Scotland. This room is where I sit to write letters: watching red-winged doves chase away scarlet-breasted finches, then balance comically on a feeder too small for them, the boat-tailed grackles drink from my malfunctioning sprinklers, the mourning doves splash wildly in the birdbath, the squirrels stretch almost beyond reach for sunflower seeds to fill their cheeks, the hummingbirds hover over the salvia blossoms or disappear into the trumpet vine, the monarch butterflies alight on the mimosa's feather-light wisps. It is in this room that I feed my most beloved friends. This room reminds me that while it was by grace that our lives were saved, it was the love of friends and the kindness of strangers along the River Clyde that sustained me there, to send me back to the desert friends by the Rio Grande who make that spared life worth living.

RIVER ROCKS AND OTHER ROCKS

EVERYWHERE I look around this arid home of mine, there are rocks. Solid rocks, small and large rocks around which cactus roots are adept at maneuvering to sustain themselves in their harsh native environment. Out my front window I can watch the sunset sky turn fiery, cascading its colors over Mount Cristo Rey and the *Sierra de Juárez*. That same blazing sky changes the gray Franklin Mountains behind my house into purple-and-pink-hued majesties. A twenty-minute drive in the spring puts me on the other side of the mountains, where I can walk along miles and miles of yellow poppy fields at their base. Rocks have a place of honor in my garden, encircling rainbow cactus, prickly pears, and century plants. Their natural and man-made scars make each of them unique. There is so much to be learned from rocks. They're good teachers. While visible scars add to their character, their hidden cores remain sound.

My home altar holds a rock carved with the Buddhist Avalokiteshvara mantra "Om Mani Padma Hum," as well as a rock brought to me from Bodh Gaya—the Buddha's site of enlightenment—by Lobsang Samten, one of my teachers. Scattered throughout my house are Zuni stone fetishes sculpted and finished with offering bundles of feathers and coral and turquoise.

In the glove compartment of my trusty twelve-year-old Subaru wagon, I carry a rock given to me by my talented and free-spirited friend EmBee. Etched and outlined in gold is the word "freedom." For this far west Texan, there is no greater freedom than driving beneath a vast expanse of sky whose clouds caress the reaches of every mountain range in sight. Like EmBee, I sometimes give people rocks for special occasions. I have given silvery black hematite with its grounding qualities in the hope that the strength within will somehow bolster the recipient through trying times. Other times they are rocks vibrant with the colors of life at its best, like labradorite with its shimmering, multifaceted rainbows, an aurora borealis you can hold in your hand. In fountains all over my house are stones I have collected on many journeys. They serve as reminders of places I have been, and the sound of the water trickling over them helps me find tranquility in the midst of routine tribulations.

If I teach because it is in my blood, my passion for rocks may also have its origins in my mother. When my mother was a little girl, her father used to wake up her and her older siblings at the crack of dawn and lift them onto the back of his buckboard to go down to the bank of the Rio Grande. There, the children would gather rocks, morning after morning, and load them in the *carretón*. After coming north to the border late in 1910, in hopes of escaping the Mexican Revolution, my grandfather bought land in the *Colonia Bellavista* in Ciudad Juárez to set up shop as a greengrocer. With the help of his children, and stronger, more able workers, he collected rock after rock for building walls. Ultimately he left my grandmother and all his children adobe dwellings that were home and then rental properties, which provided them needed income. Rock walls, with the final layer of mortar embedded with glistening shards of broken glass to keep out intruders, demarcated these properties.

On our weekly visits to my *mamacita*'s house in Juárez when I was growing up, the walls encircling the *corralón* beside her house contained the spiritedness of two generations of children. The yard was by then a depository for things no one in the family wanted, but the stories embedded in these objects kept them from being mere discards. The #10 washtub that my grandmother had put a chicken under to try to bring it back to life still bore the marks on its base where my mother had beat on it with a stick. The beating helped neither the chicken nor the tub. The one stayed dead, the other was dented permanently. For me at least, those rock walls embraced anything but a junkyard. Splintered vegetable crates, disintegrating adobes assimilating into the earth from which they had come, piles of rocks from some unfinished project, and shards of broken glass for walls yet to be raised—all of these evoked memories, some of my grandfather's workers, others of my own playground mischief. After I married and planted seedlings at my first house on the former riverbed down the valley, I brought cinderblocks cast aside in that *corralón* to edge my flower beds.

For as long as I can remember, on *Día de los Muertos*, All Souls' Day, my mother and I cut the zinnias, marigolds, and chrysanthemums from our garden, went over the Rio Grande to Juárez, and rode a bus south with others also going to the cemeteries. The bus let us off where the streets were closed to accommodate the flower sellers whose carts were piled high with yellow, white, and deep purple blossoms. We bought more *zempasúchil* and *crisantemas* along the way and joined the throngs who made the yearly pilgrimage to clean and decorate family grave sites. Little boys with buckets of scarce desert water followed us in to help with cleaning the gravestones and settling the dirt around them. First with my mother, later with John, and still later with Johnny, with scrub brushes and soap in hand, we cleaned the year's dust off the family's granite gravestone and used a broom to sweep all around the *lápida*. We pulled weeds and cleaned up garbage tossed about by the wind. All around us were families doing the same. Simple, rough-hewn wooden crosses with names and dates scratched in by hand shared the rocky soil with statues and monuments and elaborate mausoleums to honor the founding families of Juárez. If the hot sun had faded the lettering on the Lara Rey gravestone, one of us would go looking for the boys and men who carried an assortment of brushes and paint. We arranged fresh flowers in the vases, shared stories of the living and the dead with families around us, and said our prayers. Afterward, we lined up to eat corn on the cob boiled in #10 washtubs, served with an ample amount of butter, sprinkled with salt and chili powder, and peppered with cemetery dust. To satisfy our sweet tooths, we chewed all the juice out of chunks of fresh cut sugarcane. Year after year, the ritual trip connected me to those relatives who had died long before I was born, most especially to the grandfather who had brought his family to the Rio Grande border.

In time, instead of taking me down to the river's edge to collect rocks, my mother made good use of the rocks surrounding her new home on the north side of the Rio Grande. The house my father bought, only one street north from the fence marking the border, wasn't much of a house, but it faced south, toward Juárez, and with her labors my mother made it into a home. It was a small house, even for three people. Its saving grace was that it was built of adobe, insulating us from both the heat of summer and the cold of winter. The side yards were narrow, only five feet on the east side, even less on the west. In the backyard was room to expand the house, still leaving space for the chicken coops, rabbit hutches, and the lopsided shed filled with my father's accumulated junk.

In the L formed by the outside kitchen and bedroom walls,

my mother determined eventually to build on another room. She nailed together two-by-fours and with my help pieced together a frame into which we would pour a concrete foundation. Every day after I came home from second grade at Zavala School, we would take our respective buckets and move rocks from other parts of the yard into the form. Having a good number of rocks already there would save on the cost of gravel and labor. Not only that. She was clearing the way for a bigger garden, for fruit trees and more rosebushes. It just wouldn't do to let all those good rocks go to waste. When it came time to pour the cement, she worked side by side with the couple of men she had hired. And so it was that the foundation for her new room was built. I grew up in a house held together by her fix-it abilities, not my father's. For my father the philosopher, rocks were objects for study or decoration. So I could learn the types and names of rocks, he gave me rocks glued to cards with their respective labels and books on the geologic wonders of the world. In honor of their beauty, he gave me polished rocks dangling from thinly gold-plated chains, which I still have.

Years later, I came to have a house of my own, farther from the river, at the foot of the Franklins. Nearly centered in the yard was a Siberian elm with a trunk too thick to put my arms around. It and a Kadota fig bush spreading over an eight-foot circle gave me hope that things could grow here. Little did I know the challenge it would be. When I tried to plant a garden, the earth fought back with rocks. The caliche the house sat on was more rocks than dirt, some rocks the size of my head. My mother's child, I determined to dig them out and pile them in the center of the yard. And so I dug. I piled. I raked. In two years, I had enough rocks to serve as the base for a concrete slab. My mother, John, and I raked and smoothed the concrete as it came down the chute off the cement truck. On it I would put a shed, to house those things pack rats hoard, and outdoor furniture, on which to sit and enjoy the abundant shade from the elm.

Over the years, along the rock walls in my backyard I have planted dozens of rosebushes, as well as fragrant paperwhites to brighten the winter, crocuses to add color to the rocks on which they rest their purple petals, sunshine yellow daffodils to bloom in early spring, fragile bearded irises, which somehow withstand the brutal desert winds to brighten the Lenten season, and fruit trees from which to harvest succulent pears and peaches to go with our figs, so abundant in the summer. Even in the alkaline soil, many of my rosebushes have lasted more than twenty years, their roots somehow finding what sustenance they need in soil barely deeper than the rocks I'd dug out. Bulbs multiply happily, a testament to how life can flourish even with little nourishment. Cactus flowers greet the summer rains with joy.

When rain comes to the desert, we celebrate, especially when the hot, parched soil pleads for the heavens to open up. Scant summer rains and rare winter snows in the north keep our Rio Grande alive. Around the corner from my house is an arroyo. Its paths lead inward from the street to ocotillo, yuccas, and prickly pear, to desert willows and aromatic creosote. When it rains, even its rocks are transformed. It was in that arroyo that John and Johnny got to know each other. As soon as Johnny was sure-footed in his toddler walk, they donned their railroad caps and went off to explore, hand in hand. Johnny's vocabulary grew with the desire to describe his desert more vividly. Their strolls turned into hikes and got longer and longer as Johnny got older; by the time he was nine, they traveled the arroyo's full length through craggy paths, always careful not to disturb or trample. Their meanderings came to an end after the injuries sustained in Scotland, when John was no longer surefooted. Even with a cane or walking stick, he could no longer navigate the paths.

I lost my mother the year she turned eighty-one. She was full of life until six weeks before her death in July of necrotizing vasculitis, which rendered her blood vessels useless. I spent the next several months grieving to the melodies I had heard her sing throughout my life and agonizing over which of her belongings to keep or give away. I wished throughout those months of mourning that we had made the trip to San Francisco that I had promised her. Come Christmastime, I took what was left of my small family—John and Johnny—and we three went anyway, to put the sadness of the year to bed and awake to a new one. It was a city she would have loved—Victorian houses with lush gardens, green mountain vistas, ambrosial food. The ocean would have reminded her of my father.

On the first day of the new year, we got on a Gray Line bus and set off down the Pacific Coast Highway to visit Steinbeck country, the Monterey Peninsula. I do not remember much about the trip until a rock hit the window beside where Johnny and I were sitting. It must have been a good-sized one because it shattered the safety glass, obliterating our view and leaving pieces of glass precariously loose. The bus driver pulled over to survey the damage and to make sure we were all right. On our right was Pigeon Point Lighthouse, built in 1875. Nothing in the bus driver's manual seemed to address such incidents, so we improvised. John's heavy cane served to knock out the window so the chunks of glass wouldn't fly as we drove to Davenport Landing to await a new bus. To block the wind, we retrieved one of several giant plastic sheets that were littering the shoreline, but there was nothing on the bus to hold it. Together, Johnny and I held up the plastic, he leaning on the bottom edge and I balancing myself against it over his head. The other passengers seemed mostly oblivious to our efforts to keep the chilly wind out of their eyes.

Only one person made eye contact with me as I shifted positions from time to time to give my arms a rest from the contortionist pose. When we stopped at Davenport Landing for lunch, she came over to thank me and to ask if she could join us. I was captivated immediately by her bright eyes and the French lilt in her voice. Paulette Dupré was seventy and traveling alone, back from Tahiti where she had visited her daughter. This was her first trip to the States; she was spending only two days on the coast and was staying in the Hotel Chancellor, as were we. Over French onion soup she told us briefly about her Réunion Island birthplace, her life in Nîmes with her professor husband and their four children, her own teaching career, and her summer country home in Gaverlac. Before the meal was even half done, she extended an invitation for us to come see her, and we exchanged addresses and phone numbers. By the time the new bus arrived to take us to Carmel-by-the-Sea, we were a foursome. We visited Mission San Carlos Borromeo and spent the rest of our day trip together, then took a bay cruise the following morning. We bade Paulette farewell after a long brunch at the Canterbury Hotel amidst the hanging ferns.

And so it was that we found ourselves "a stone's throw away" from a second European adventure. Within a week of our homecoming, Paulette sent travel brochures describing Nîmes and wrote to say her invitation was heartfelt. I waited up one night until it was a decent hour in France and called her, still in disbelief that anyone would invite three strangers from Texas into her home. Since our ill-fated first attempt to see Europe eight years before, we had not ventured overseas. I had saved up enough to try again, and the trip scheduled for that summer was extended by several days so we could visit Paulette. The one request she had of us was that we not bring much luggage, since her tiny Peugeot would have room for little more than ourselves.

On these pages I share Paulette with you, tell you of her life, sometimes in her words, written for me as a birthday gift on thick linen paper in her polished schoolteacher's script. Of her childhood on Réunion Island, she writes, "I have few punctual or precise memories of my first years on this earth. We lived in the country, amidst the sugar-cane fields, 2 kilometers away from the village (now called Domenjod, but then known as 'Riviere des Pluies,' the river of rains, probably because it was very often dry except in the rainy season)." She was born in 1921 and lived in a "primitive" house built before the French Revolution. Her father enlarged it with a "spacious verandah in front and two wings, one containing a sitting room and a bedroom, the other a dining room and a kitchen." There were no modern conveniences, but still, she says, "we all lived there in full happiness, far from the noise of the town." The long drive to the house was lined with rosebushes that "bloomed in glory in the summer."

When she turned five, she began walking the two miles beside her sisters to attend the village Catholic school run by local nuns. She took her First Communion in the parish church where she had been christened by Father Antoine Bourbonnais, a French missionary priest. For twelve years she went to school, her Sundays "punctuated by a cinema show" when "Daddy, who by now had a car came and fetched us from town for the 'family day.'" Paulette and her sisters spent summer holidays, in January and February, on the estate (which could be reached only in her father's lorry) and the August winter holiday by the seaside in Saint-Gilles, on the west coast.

"Then came the thunder in the blue sky—the war!" she writes. It broke out the year she completed her secondary studies, so she could not go to France to continue her studies at the university. The following six years she stayed home with her sister Mado, who took sewing lessons. Paulette began gardening, and "with the help of an old Indian called Casimir, looked after the 212 rosebushes" that lined the drive to the house. She also created a vegetable garden; the first money she ever earned "came from the selling of the vegetables" she had grown herself. In 1946, the war over, she sailed to France and, as "an old student of 25" began studying English at Montpellier University. Her much beloved father gave her a bicycle after she passed the first part of her university degree, and in the summer of 1947 she and two of her male classmates donned shorts and cycled up the mountains from Perpignan to Le Boulou to the Spanish frontier. They left their bicycles on the French side of the border and walked past the guards into town with no problem. When they came back, however, the guards tried to arrest her, for in Franco's Spain women in shorts were not allowed. An argument ensued, and her companions had to convince the border guards that she was a very proper young woman, not a "hussy" (her word) despite her attire. She was released into their care after they promised to leave Spain immediately. Paulette tells this story with a gleam in her eye. She graduated in two years, then spent a year in Brighton in Sussex as the French-language assistant at Varndean School for girls, living with the Bowis family, whose son John is now a member of the European Parliament. From there she went to a teaching job in Ajaccio in Corsica, then went back to read for the *agrégation* at the Sorbonne.

At thirty she met Guy, a history and geography teacher, who became her husband. They lived first in Thionville in Lorraine near Alsace, then applied for positions in Réunion and went there for two years, where Cécile and Brigitte were born. Guy was "not too keen on living in Réunion," so they settled in Nîmes, in a house not in the "posh" old part of town, but on the "other side of the tracks" where Paulette found a house to her liking, a house with a front garden whose high stone walls came to be covered with wisteria vines, and a rear garden where she still

Paulette with her bicycle, the summer of 1947,
wearing the shorts that got her arrested in Spain.

grows her spectacular peonies and passion vines. Guy taught all his life in the school where he had been a student. Their sons François and Bruno were born in Nîmes. She lost Guy to a ruptured aneurysm in 1989; Paulette herself survived the cancer that followed the shock of his sudden death. She has also had back surgery and a hip replacement, neither of which has dimmed the sparkle of her love for life.

To visit Paulette's Gaverlac summer home is to visit Paradise. It is one home of four in a hamlet in the south of France, in the province of Rouergue in L'Aveyron, next door to a farm whose ewes produce milk for *Societé Roquefort*. The bells around their necks announce their morning departures to and evening returns from the fields. Paulette bought and restored the seventeenth-century white sandstone farmhouse after her father's death. The roof is constructed of *lauze*, a thick slate used only in that area in

France. A dried *cardabelle* hangs on the heavy wooden door to welcome visitors. At the top of a short outdoor flight of stairs is her kitchen, the heart of this house. On one end, under the staircase, is a built-in bed, an alcove, with thick red curtains to keep out the cold.

The focal point of the kitchen is a roomwide fireplace, its hearth a perfect spot for sipping the Chateau Margaux Bordeaux still made by her father's family five kilometers from his birthplace, or her homemade Tiger's Milk, both delightful aperitifs. A cast-iron pot swings into the fire for cooking. Rough-hewn benches provide seating for guests at Paulette's table, a magnificent old piece, with drawers to store cutlery and *serviettes* kept in cut-work, hand-embroidered linen cases made by nuns in the village of Cilaos in Réunion. Against another wall sits a worktable; removing its top reveals a trough in which to knead bread dough. Above, a rack holds plates from countries she has visited. The windows look out onto her well-tended vegetable garden where she picks artichokes off bushes that tower over her, where she grows strawberries succulent with a faint but distinct taste of lavender, and raspberries that she turns into preserves glistening with the light of liquid rubies. For me, a girl of the desert, whose outdoor childhood greenery consisted of what my mother could nurture in our five-foot-wide stretch of earth, Paulette's Gaverlac is indeed Paradise. When I see Paulette in her garden, or in her kitchen, I see my mother.

There seems to be no daytime noise in Gaverlac, save the bells of the ewes, the occasional barking of sheepdogs keeping their charges in line, and birdsong. In a courtyard outside the kitchen there are dahlias, hydrangeas, and clematis vines. In June, the countryside surrounding the house is awash in the sunshine gold of blooming Spanish broom and the many shades of green in the well-kept farm fields stretching everywhere to the horizon.

Paulette spends from July through September in her paradise, welcoming visitors from all over the world, her summer culminating for many years in a gathering of her Club 21, fellow teachers from her secondary school who were all born in 1921. Alas, that gathering has dwindled with their hesitation to drive the 200 kilometers from Nîmes.

Our days there began not with alarm clocks but with a gentle light coming through the windows to wake us up—except for those mornings when aromas from Paulette's kitchen roused us first. After picking raspberries one afternoon, Paulette made preserves at dawn, and by the time we wandered into the kitchen, jars lined up neatly on the hearth sparkled in the sun's early rays. The simplicity of life at Gaverlac is nothing short of elegant. We helped with the gardening and fruit picking, read a little, visited a bit with the neighbors. One afternoon after an evening rain, she gathered up baskets, one for each of us, and took us driving as far as the road allowed. When we got out of the car, she led us into the boggy woods to go mushroom picking for *cèpes* and *girolles*. As she told us what to look for and how to identify the safe mushrooms from the not-so-safe ones, she also warned us to listen for wild boars. We encountered none and gathered a good harvest, the most succulent dinner-plate-size mushroom eliciting gleeful squeals from Paulette. True to her country ways, by the time we woke up the next morning, she had already cooked and canned them and designated some for us to take home. The woods have been felled but the taste of those mushrooms and the excitement of the search linger in our memories.

Paulette has a sense of merriment and adventure that is both charming and exciting. If she saw wild strawberries along the road beyond a little stream, she would pull over, pull out a basket from the trunk, straddle the stream, and pick them. On our first visit to France, she took us to Aubrac, a stop on the pilgrimage to

Santiago de Campostello, showing us the eleventh-century bridge over the River Le Lot by Espalion.

At *Chez Germaine*, surrounded by families with dogs making the pilgrimage, we savored course after course of what Paulette pronounced "ordinary food": pâtés and sausages made by the village butchers and vegetables grown as close by as the restaurant's backyard. The crowning glory of the meal was a diadem of *aligot*, buttered mashed potatoes combined with cheese no older than three days—*la tomme*—made nineteen kilometers from Laguiole, a mixture that ceremoniously came to encircle our heads. We knew then the secret surprise that Paulette had been holding in. While this mashed potato ring was being placed on our heads, we didn't give a second thought as to whether or not it would stick to our hair. In fact, it came off easily. The *aligot* was as

Paulette straddling a stream to pick wild strawberries on a road in the Province of Rouergue, in the south of France.

delicious as the crowning was playful, all part of the *Chez Germaine* experience.

At Millau, on a shopping expedition, she showed us where the Tarn River flows through the magnificent Gorges du Tarn. Everywhere she took us in France, there seemed to be rivers banked with beautiful green spaces. And everywhere we went, we took pictures of Paulette by rivers, in the same way that we had done for my mother.

Near the end of that first visit to France, Paulette agreed to come to Texas the following year. Living where far west Texas touches New Mexico and Mexico, we have always loved the drive from El Paso to Santa Fe. I planned a two-week trip along that route and equipped my just-purchased Subaru wagon with assorted pillows in case Paulette needed to nap from time to time. Paulette arrived in El Paso in mid-May of 1993 armed with the two cameras she carries everywhere and, of course, her diary. In her house in Nîmes is a bookcase devoted to, at last count, eighty-four albums with labeled photos from every journey she has taken and the diaries she has kept since 1951.

From El Paso to Albuquerque, we four—John, Johnny, Paulette, and I—roughly followed the Rio Grande's upstream course. In Santa Fe we focused on historic buildings, most especially the Miraculous Staircase in the Loretto Chapel and the cathedral that towers next to it. From there we went to the *Santuario de Chimayó*, famous for its healing soil. A devoted Catholic, Paulette loves visiting churches and speaks fondly still of Chimayó. She, like my mother, scooped up a handful of sacred dirt.

Moving northward, we crossed the San Juan River into Colorado. At Durango, we boarded the train on the narrow gauge railroad. Pulled by a steam engine, we spent the day winding through the beautiful San Juan Mountains, the Animas River keeping us company along the way. Paulette's delight at every sight and sound reminded me of my mother's when we had taken her on the same trip.

We drove back to El Paso through Lincoln National Forest, stopping at the Mescalero Apache Reservation's Inn of the Mountain Gods, where the Ruidoso River and the man-made lake outside our room's picture window enchanted Paulette. In our ten days on the road, Paulette took not so much as a short nap for fear of missing something. After we returned to El Paso, our closest friends joined us for a farewell dinner. And of course Paulette invited everyone to visit her in France.

Two friends did accompany me the following year: Ruth, my friend and confidante for over thirty years, and her daughter April, then eleven. Nîmes and Gaverlac became a different world when Paulette invited her daughter Brigitte and her grandchildren Arnaud, Charlie, and Fleur to go along on our excursions, this time in Brigitte's big station wagon. In Nîmes, we shared a meal of guinea hen, exquisitely prepared, accompanied by an assortment of fresh vegetables and crusty bread. The following day Paulette put a picnic basket together with the leftovers, several kinds of cheeses, and wine. Off we went zipping through the countryside once more, this time in the *Valle de la Dourbie* to a spot near the village of Cantobre. There, we unloaded the car, walked a bit down to the bank of the river, spread out blankets, and had a most sumptuous picnic, all the while watching the children play together, although April spoke no French and Brigitte's children only a bit of English. Irrepressible Charlie, five at the time, saw no need to keep on his clothes when he went wading in the Dourbie, a tributary of the Tarn.

Cécile joined us to see Camargue, home of the famous horses and bulls, where the Rhône feeds the earth, where pink flamingos wander freely, and where the fields of giant sunflowers are too amazing to describe. I waded in the Mediterranean as my mother waded in every water she came across. The final outing of that trip we enjoyed a multicourse dinner served on the *Emmanuel 3* as it circled Lac de Pareloup. Finding a bit of quiet time with Paulette, I asked if she wanted to come to Texas and New Mexico again. She said no, that the world was far too big and she was getting too old to visit a place twice. I said I would meet her anywhere she wanted to go. She decided on Canada—she wanted to see all of Canada, in the fall when the leaves would be at their most glorious—and trusted the planning of the trip to me.

Wow. All of Canada, I thought. How do I do this? With the help of a wonderful travel agent named Angela McDiarmit at Brewster's Tours in Banff, it was easy. I picked historic Canadian Pacific Railroad hotels anywhere they were available, and Angela, enchanted by my tales of Paulette, saw to it that every room had a spectacular view. Paulette had one very specific request about our trip—that we have our breakfasts in our room. We did. Every morning began with fresh croissants and fruit. We started out in Vancouver and went by bus north through the Canadian Rockies, listened to the songs of the loons at Lac Le Jeune Resort in Kamloops, experienced a snowfall in Banff, and were awestruck with the incredibly beautiful view of Lake Louise from our room. Together, we walked carefully on the Athabascan Glacier. At Jasper Park Lodge the tour director warned us not to get too close to the doors or windows of our cabin if we heard any unusual noises because it was mating season for the elk. Still, we managed a quiet walk along the Athabasca River when the elk rested. The train took us across the Canadian plains to a stop beneath the Royal York Hotel in Toronto. We donned Smurf-colored hooded raincoats and saw Niagara Falls from a Maid of the Mist cruise ship. Montreal and Quebec gave us views of the St. Lawrence River, not to mention meals that were almost as delicious as Paulette's. The Laurentian Mountains displayed for us their brilliant hues of golden, orange, and red maple leaves. Twenty-one days we spent together, sharing mountains and rivers. Then Paulette returned to Nîmes in time to celebrate her seventy-fourth birthday.

Six years later, in 2001, Johnny and I returned to France to see Paulette. Once again, she asked us to travel light. We took the fast train—the TGV—from Paris to Avignon, where she picked us up. There was very little room in the Peugeot for luggage. In her trunk were several big baskets of beautiful, fresh strawberries for preserves. On the terrace overlooking her garden and the street in Nîmes she fed us crusty bread, salad, and pâté made from pork fed solely on acorns. We ate at Bel Castel beside the Aveyron River, where I gathered some rocks to take home, saw the forti- fied stone church at Isnieres by the Viaur River, and climbed to the top of the fortress church of Sainte-Radegonde. The Gaverlac paradise was just as we remembered, peaceful and quiet.

For excitement, Cécile took us to a Roman coliseum in Nîmes, where bullfights date back to the Roman Empire. Cécile, who knew the breeders, could answer all of Johnny's questions about bullfighting. Later, when Johnny ran with the bulls over the cobblestoned streets, I did not tag along to take pictures. I'm not sure I could have kept the camera steady. I treasure all the pic- tures taken on that trip, but the grandest one of Johnny is on the Pont du Gard, the Roman aqueduct built about 50 AD. Nîmes's water supply once came from the Eure spring at the base of Uzès. The Gardon River flows beneath it. Between Nîmes and Avignon, the Pont du Gard's stone arches are at their most beau- tiful, the aqueduct's three stories most intact.

Since our trip to Canada, Paulette has been—on her own—to Iceland and Zimbabwe, followed Paul and John's footsteps in Greece and Ephesus, returned to Réunion with her son Bruno, and most recently, for her eighty-second birthday, had her first gondola ride in Venice with her son François, his wife, Anne-Marie, and their children, Paul and Hugo. In 2004, she and I traveled together once more, to Austria, where, twenty years after the car wreck in Scotland, I saw the Salzburg hills. Paulette, of course, made new friends on the tour bus and invited them to Gaverlac.

At eighty-three, petite Paulette looks like a pixie, with her very short-cropped snow-white hair, her laughing eyes, and mischievous smile. She has boundless energy: in the kitchen, preparing her so-called simple dishes that my palate will never forget, in her gardens, trying to outsmart the rabbits who also find her fresh vegetables delicious, embroidering for friends old and new, knitting warm blankets to comfort the poor in the winter. From that first day at Pigeon Point Lighthouse, as I still mourned for my mother, she has taught me how to be like the sunflowers of Camargue—always reaching for the light.

On my latest visit to Nîmes, I spent quiet days alone with Paulette for the first time since Canada. She let me help her make strawberry preserves and prepare the garden for her absence while we went to Austria. Watering her back garden early one morning, I noticed something I never had before: mint was growing beside the wood violets, just as it did in my mother's garden, and just as it does in mine. Rocks smoothed by the flow of river water form paths between flower beds. I chose three to add to my fountains at home, tokens of the tranquility of Nîmes and my time there with Paulette.

THE SACRED RIVER GANGES

HOWEVER MUCH I am my mother's daughter, I am anything but fearless. I grew up in such a cocooned environment that I was married before I had spent so much as an evening alone, and my fear of the dark was equaled only by my terror of night driving. Even in the daytime, I was cowed by the prospect of driving the forty miles to Las Cruces, the next town to the west. At forty-five, I had never taken so much as a short trip without some member of my family. I might not have to this day had it not been for Johnny.

Johnny was nineteen and about to leave home on his first quest for independence. Not happy pursuing an education after high school, he decided to move away, not only from El Paso, but from Texas altogether. Loving the ocean, and coffee, he had opted for Seattle, to become an expert coffee maker, a *barista*. A child with an inner drumbeat so strong that we were frequently at odds, Johnny was forever testing my parenting skills. I wanted to be the kind of mother who never raised her voice. That was not realistic. We are both strong willed. He had me reaching early on for the wisdom of Gibran, compelling me to acknowledge that you may give children "your love but not your thoughts

. . . strive to be like them, but seek not to make them like you . . . for life goes not backward nor tarries with yesterday." I became his mother with three hours notice when he was two months old, and we grew up together. I will always wonder whether he has learned as much from me as I have from him.

One of the wisest things he ever did was introduce me to the Chenrezig Tibetan Buddhist Culture Center. It is interesting to me that Johnny, who never really knew his grandfather's affinity for Eastern religions and thought, would come to study them before me. It is because of Johnny that I realized, long after my father's death, the full impact that Eastern philosophy had on him, how all those years of yoga and Buddhist writings had enriched my father's life. It was Johnny who first found at the Chenrezig Center the value of silence, of being quiet with his thoughts. He saw that I needed to be still with mine. He chastised me regularly for not taking time to read more, to write, to be more than a mother to him and a caregiver to John. I am not in my father's league in his dedication to study and self-reflection, but I continue to use meditation to find my balance, to keep my center through daily challenges. I became involved in the Chenrezig Center's activities alongside Johnny, and soon I was feeding Tibetan monks who came through El Paso on the way to speaking and musical performances in northern New Mexico or California. As my father's life was blessed by attending classes taught by the Hindu sage Rishi Sherval, who had studied with monks in Tibet, my life is blessed with the opportunity to be of service to Tibetan monks who come through the desert. Their gentleness continues to have an effect on me.

It was those connections to Buddhism that drew my attention to a two-and-a-half-inch sidebar in the *El Paso Times* in the summer of 1994. The boldface heading read "Travel opportunity." Rotary clubs in New Mexico and West Texas, seeking to "improve international understanding of people from different countries," were looking for volunteers to participate in a group study tour to India and Nepal, places I'd longed to see. So I cut out the item and taped it on my refrigerator. Following Rotary procedures, I got the application and found a club to sponsor me. Days came and went, and I didn't fill out the application, certain that my professional resume was too weak to impress anyone. All the years Johnny was growing up, I had done mostly volunteer work—at the Lighthouse for the Blind, with children at University Presbyterian Church, and short stints across the border in a Juárez *colonia* directing Vacation Bible School. My first full-time job was the one I had at the time, as executive director of Latch Key Centers, a social service agency dedicated to providing after-school care for children in the *Segundo Barrio*.

Finally Johnny led me through the paperwork and helped me fill it out. The application had to be hand delivered to a club sponsor in order to secure the proper signatures before mailing to the project's coordinator. When my car would not start on the afternoon the application was due (was I not my father's daughter?), we chugalugged in Johnny's '63 VW bug and made it with only five minutes to spare. Group Study Exchange Coordinator Dan Schulte invited me to interview for the GSE Team—to comprise one Rotarian and four non-Rotarians from Texas and New Mexico—in September. When I was accepted, Johnny was overjoyed. Shortly before he boarded a train for Seattle, he and I spent the weekend together in Ruidoso. On the way back, after a light rain that came down from the mountains, a double rainbow appeared in our path. We took that as a good sign for our respective journeys.

Mine began with smaller forays to GSE training sessions, round-trips of 200 to 400 miles. Ruth, I'm sure, would have accompanied me. But having decided that I had no business crossing the world on my own if I could not cross a neighboring state, I drove alone. From the training sessions I learned about the breadth and depth of work that Rotary does worldwide, and about what I could expect to find in India, including the tremendous poverty that many Westerners, we were told, found difficult to handle. India, they warned us, was in the midst of a cholera epidemic. I knew that Juárez was as well. I would be traveling with a Rotarian leader, Bob Entrop from Roswell, New Mexico, and non-Rotarians Suzy Baldwin from Gallup, Philip Menicucci from Albuquerque, and Mark Steffen from Las Cruces. I was the only El Pasoan, picked perhaps for my background in social service—and primarily on the basis of my interview, for my original application had somehow gone missing.

While my journey to India would hardly be akin to that of Dervla Murphy, who, as she recounts in *Full Tilt,* traveled alone from Dublin to Delhi on a bicycle, for me it would certainly be conquering. For the first time in my entire life I would be just Lucy, not anyone's daughter, wife, or mother. I left home not knowing where I would be from day to day, not able to provide phone numbers where I could be contacted easily. It was a giant leap of faith. All I knew was that I was going first to Calcutta.

Getting to Calcutta was an adventure in itself. I had packed a carry-on bag with essentials and a very large suitcase filled with assorted gifts for people I would meet. Albuquerque, New Mexico, was our team's meeting point. As I pulled the overstuffed monster suitcase off the conveyor in the Albuquerque airport, it slipped, landed on my sandaled right foot, and split the big toe wide open. An embarrassing amount of blood gushed onto a clean floor. I thought, Uh oh, this must be an omen—and wondered if I should be taking a split toe to a country with sometimes contaminated water. I would contract something deadly on the first day, before I got to see any of India. When the plane could not take off from Albuquerque because it was snowing, I wondered further about the wisdom of this journey. When the flight in Phoenix was also grounded—this time because of heavy rain in Los Angeles, an Eeyore-esque gloom began to descend on me. I thought again that something in El Paso had too strong a grip on me, that this trip was not meant to be. When, owing to these delays, we missed our plane in Los Angeles altogether, I made two phone calls, one to Johnny in Washington, another to Ruth in New Mexico. Should I heed these omens, I asked, and go back? My oracles both issued resounding no's. My fears relieved by their confidence, I took off. What with time zone changes and layovers between one plane and another, I lost track of the hours we spent en route. I do remember napping under showers of orchids in the Singapore airport and buying my first souvenirs in Bangkok. On the long flight there, I started the only journal I have ever kept. No matter how long our days were, it was important to record what I saw, did, and felt during those seven weeks on my own.

We landed in Calcutta's Dum Dum Airport a full day after we had been expected; the welcoming reception the Rotarians had prepared had taken place without us. The Brazilian Group Study Exchange Team, who was to be there during our first four weeks, had gotten all the attention. Our only greeters were somber guards in drab green, gripping firearms that looked old but nonetheless menacing. I was more than a little spooked as we were herded rather brusquely along in lines with the other passengers. Once the Rotarians arrived, we could all relax. In no time, we were at the head of the queue. Palms placed together, heads slightly bowed, our hosts greeted us with the traditional "Namastay," meaning roughly "The Divinity in me salutes the Divinity in you." We had been told our welcome might be more reserved than what we were accustomed to on the comforting *abrazo*-giving border. Yet the hugs and kisses and everyone talking at once put me in mind of the joyful *convivios* of the Mexican schoolteachers. I knew then that I was in the right place. The ten pieces of luggage the team had checked in Albuquerque had not arrived with us, but I had enough in my carry-on to be presentable for several days. After what seemed like an eternity filling out forms in triplicate to track our suitcases, we finally got our first glimpse of Calcutta. It was as if we'd stepped into a grainy, worn print of a classic black-and-white movie. Everything I'd read about Calcutta was true—the grime, the poverty, the traffic. Calcutta was both exciting and frightening.

Through air nearly black with pollution, in an atmosphere filled with unfamiliar sights and smells and the honking of drivers all around, Rotarian Indranil Biswas dropped Suzy and me at what in my somnolent state I took to be a boarding house. In the first beds we'd seen in two days, she and I fell into restless half-sleep, wondering where we really were and whether anyone would be back for us in the morning. Walking on the walls and strolling on the high ceilings were sticky-footed lizards whose bodies cast occasional Godzilla-like shadows. To look after us, there were two male attendants, one with a white beard down to his waist and neither of whom spoke English. Bless their poor souls. When they knocked in the middle of the night with a snack for us, we were too terrified to open the door and let them in. I'm not sure whether they were more afraid of us or we of them.

The scavenger birds began their daylight calling first; these crows were sleek with a gray shield on their chests. Below our window there was a vacant garbage-laden lot and men relieving themselves in plain sight. Across the street was a building either in the midst of construction or in serious disrepair. It was difficult to tell which. There were men cooking on makeshift stoves on the floor of various stories in this open building, tin braziers like the ones at the Juárez market. Clothes had been hung out to dry on steel beams. There were other birds, too, chirping much like the sparrows in my Siberian elm at home. At dawn they supplied a comforting contrast to the honking that never ceased, day or night. In the morning, our attendants looked downright friendly, not ominous at all. It's amazing what even a short night's sleep and a quick shower can do for one's outlook. We discovered we were in a guesthouse belonging to the company of a Rotarian host (though I never learned the name of either).

Separated from the rest of our team at the airport and unable to communicate with our attendants, Suzy and I had no idea what we were supposed to do on our first day. Bob found us, though, and asked that we be ready within the hour to begin our ambassadorial responsibilities. Our Rotarian hostesses for the day gave us a history and culture lesson as we drove through the traffic. West Bengal is situated just above the Bay of Bengal in eastern India. Here, the mighty River Ganges breaks up into dozens of rivers and rivulets before it flows into the sea. It is a sacred river both to Buddhists and Hindus. Calcutta, the capital of Bengal, in 1995 was inhabited by more than 10 million people, with a floating population of another 2 to 3 million. This floating population came from rural villages to seek a better life in the city, just as people cross the Rio Grande into El Paso hoping for the same. Through what can only be described as chaotic congestion, wooden bullock carts tote freshly published books, brightly decorated trucks creak along piled high with every conceivable tropical fruit, and rickshaws fueled by barefooted men carry people to and fro. Chauffeured limousines share the road with cars held together by duct tape, and rusted double-decker buses tilt with the weight of passengers packed like the proverbial sardines. Vespa scooters carry entire families, women's saris flowing in the hot breezes. Men and women alike carry tremendous loads on their heads. Cows garlanded in orange and yellow marigolds wander the sidewalks scrounging for food. Women pat cow dung into patties, then slap them on walls to dry so they can be used for fuel. Thousands of people have no toilet facilities. Wages then were 30–50 rupees per day (31 rupees equaled one U.S. dollar). Two thousand Rupees yearly was considered poverty level, and 40 percent of people lived on less than that. The poverty in the streets of Calcutta resembled the poverty I see still across the Rio Grande every day, the poverty I saw close-up for several years working summers in the *colonias* of the hills of Juárez. In Calcutta I was surrounded by it, traveling through it daily going from one Rotary function to another. The contrast between the stark street scenes and the opulent hotels where some of the meetings were held was dramatic.

Dramatic as well were the Rotary District 3290 projects that we participated in during our seven-week trip. Our first morning we snailed our way in traffic to a woman's health initiative, where Suzy and I spent the morning recording babies' weights and packaging vitamins for new mothers. The Rotary Club Metropolitan's Legs for Legless project housed in a basement facility the equipment and staff with which to build wooden limbs and provide them at a cost of US$20, a sum unreachable for many, except for the generosity of club members and visitors like us. Rotarian women taught village girls elaborate embroidery techniques, sold their linens, and returned the money to the village. There were rural projects as far away as 150 kilometers as well as urban projects right in the middle of the city. Gandhi could have been speaking of Rotarians when he said, "Service which is rendered without joy helps neither the servant nor the served. But all other pleasures and possessions pale into nothingness before service which is rendered in a spirit of joy." Every day we visited different sites and attended Rotary Club meetings held all across the city, some in the very proper clubs built by the British. Our team did presentations, in which we shared our Southwestern culture, our way of life, our careers. The agency I ran in El Paso served children living in the *Segundo Barrio*, the third poorest zip code zone in the United States. I knew firsthand the struggles involved in meeting the needs of families living in poverty.

We stayed with Rotary families all but a few days of our seven-week stint, relocating every five or six days. The second weekend we were there, however, we were housed at the Sharani Lodge with the other five-person team in Calcutta at that time, one from Brazil. It was the only time that all ten of us, Brazilians and Americans, were together under one roof, and it was a boisterous, happy time. The Sharani was a very small establishment, with only a few rooms up a steep but mercifully short staircase. I got my introduction to Indian bathroom facilities at the Sharani—two elevated concrete steps above a hole, with a faucet coming out of a nearby wall and a tin can within reach. In case you don't quite get the picture, toilet protocol dictated that the utilized spot be rinsed clean and readied for the next user. Having a bath required advance notice to the front desk, unless you were a really hardy cold-water–loving soul. An attendant would carry up hot water in five-gallon buckets. You half-filled one empty bucket with cold water out of a waist-high faucet, poured hot water into it, and used a tin can to then pour lukewarm water over yourself to lather and later rinse. Come to think of it, it was not much different from my childhood experience of heating water in a big pot and pouring it into the metal tub that already had cold water in it.

That weekend, team members were introduced as honored visitors at the district conference and each was given several bouquets of red roses and tuberose, as we would soon find out was customary. Back at the Sharani, lacking vases for our bouquets,

*Lucy packaging vitamins for new mothers
at a Rotarian Women's Health Initiative in Calcutta, 1995.*

we giddily scattered rose petals and aromatic tuberose buds in one another's rooms. Except for Luciana Martins, a stunning dark-haired beauty, the Brazilians spoke very little English and conversations were limited. Instead they sang for us, and danced in the hallways. Our team was not particularly talented. The only song we could sing, poorly at that, was "Home on the Range," hardly suitable for dancing.

We ten did almost everything together, including get lost in the middle of the night. Somehow on Saturday night we became separated from our host Rotarians. Anxious to get back to the lodge, we decided to walk, but soon discovered that all the buildings looked alike. Around the neighborhood we wandered—for what felt like hours—through dark streets with no landmarks we could distinguish, carrying our bouquets like beauty pageant contestants on a runway. I began to feel as apprehensive as I did foolish; every cent I had brought with me for the trip was in my purse. Fortunately we were walking in a circle and wound up back at the conference center, where our hosts found us and took us home. Sunday night, after a shopping spree at a leather fair, our team had another occasion to find our way home sans Rotarians. That night, following advice in some travel book I'd read, we hailed a cab and handed the driver the Sharani's card so he would know where to take us. The book's fallacy was in overlooking the many dialects spoken and scripts used in Calcutta, not to mention the high rate of illiteracy. Our poor driver could make nothing of the card, but between his patience with our sign language and our increased attention to landmarks, we made it back.

After a week in the city's torpor-inducing air, both teams welcomed the opportunity to visit a rural village where the Rabindra Sarobar Club had put their projects into place. By bus, we inched out of Calcutta, through the suffocating traffic and incessant honking, leaving behind countless sidewalk stands selling everything from food to custom-made clothes, and traveled 120 kilometers south along the River Ganges to the village of Ullan. The cows on the road looked healthier the farther we got from the city; the pollution gave way to sunshine and to air we breathed in hungrily. Women in rice fields along the road tended their crops. When the bus stopped, it seemed as though we had been transported into a *National Geographic* foldout. Serenaded by birds overhead, we meandered down a road of yellow bricks made and put in place by nearby villagers, past mud huts with thatched roofs and now and then snakes hanging from trees. A loudspeaker broke above the sounds of the birds to announce the first match in a cricket tournament.

Around the curve, however, were not the cricket players and their fans, but the entire population of the village. Hundreds of men, women, and children, dressed in their finest clothes, had lined the last part of the walkway. With palms together, they

Lucy offering a Namastay greeting to a
Bengali girl at Ullan, south of Calcutta, 1995.

greeted us with a chorus of "Namastay." It was beautiful and humbling. At the village entrance were little girls in traditional gold and red Bengali dress, their faces filigreed in intricate white scrollwork. The girls presented us with straw hats to keep the sun at bay, and we bent our heads so that a dot of sandalwood paste could be placed on our foreheads, the *ashirbad,* a Bengali blessing. So anointed, we sloshed through the mud to watch the end of a cricket match, which I struggled but failed to figure out. Uttam Ganguli and his fellow club members then gave us a tour of their Ullan projects; together with the villagers, they had made bricks for the road that had taken us to the village as well as for a building that served both as a school and medical facility. Teachers and doctors, also sponsored by their club, made regular trips to Ullan.

In preparation for lunch, we were led into a courtyard by a pond where a young man held a pitcher of water, handed us soap and a towel, and helped us wash our hands. We removed our shoes at the doorway to an open-air pavilion, and sat cross-legged on mats to be served a traditional Bengali meal eaten on sal leaf plates, the rural equivalent of the aluminum *thali* that I was used to in Calcutta. Though I recognized dal (yellow lentils in this case), a staple in Bengali cuisine, the *batis* (bowls) placed in a circle around our mound of rice held strange and wonderful culinary delights—a sweet fish called *rohi, alu posto bhaja* (fried potatoes with poppy seeds), *patha mangsha jhol* (mutton with gravy), and a sweet tomato and kissmiss chutney. The banana leaf placemats kept the floor clean. Dessert was *mishti doi* (sweet yogurt) and *rassagullas* (white pastry balls in syrup, also called *barfis* or *burfis*). All these juicy concoctions we ate with our right hands, minus silverware, slurping judiciously so as to not make messes of ourselves. Our struggling attempts at etiquette provided considerable entertainment for the villagers who gathered to watch us eat.

Picture my mother surrounded by children and you can picture me in the middle of the jungle wriggling restlessly on a folding chair, not content to be merely a part of the audience as we waited for the next part of the children's program to begin. I asked Uttam to translate while I tried to teach the youngest girls a song. We sat together, Uttam, these children, and I, in the afternoon sun, attempting to break through language barriers to sing "The Eensy-Weensy Spider." Afterward, as a bright orange ball of a sun set over the jungle and the moon rose, we sipped sweet tea out of clay *peeky putts.*

The week after our visit to Ullan, I lived with the Gupta family in Calcutta: Hari, active in the Rotary Club of Calcutta, Shakuntula, his wife, Rashmi, their daughter-in-law, Saurabh, their grandson, and Devpriya, their granddaughter. In the mornings I awakened to a light tap on my door and a tray of "bed tea," dark Darjeeling tea from the Indian mountainside, sweetened with sugar and lightened with hot milk—and served with a

Lucy with Bengali girls in the village of Ullan, 1995.

cookie or two. As I sipped, I could smell the incense placed daily on a family altar to Ganesh, the Elephant God. The quiet of the morning gave me ample opportunity to do my own meditations. After showering, I joined the Guptas for breakfast on the terrace, which overlooks a garden, as Paulette's does in Nîmes. On the center of a silver *thali* was an oven-hot deep dish with mushroom gravy toast. Surrounding it were *batis* filled with nuts, sprouts, dates, fresh papaya, and yogurt. In this household, nothing was hurried. Tranquility flooded every corner of the house.

Shakuntula let me observe the making of *papad*, a crispy waferlike sun-dried bread made yearly; Rashmi and I spent time on the roof while she worked on her prize-winning bonsai; Saurabh, a serious and studious young man, visited politely. It was Devpriya, eight at the time, who spent the most time with me, testing my knowledge of knock-knock jokes at every opportunity. I sang children's songs for her in Spanish and English, and she sang and danced for me. Hari made sure that I was on time to Rotary activities. His club had been in existence since 1920. One of its projects, the annual Children's Treat Day, begun in 1925, was by 1995 serving 1,200 orphan children from twenty-five institutions. The days were full—attending conferences, speaking at club meetings, helping with one project or another. But always, before getting ready for the evening activities, there was high tea at five o'clock. It was Rashmi who taught me how to wrap a sari with no pins, a part of the cultural experience of being in India. On Friday night, I attended my first wedding with the Guptas, dressed in a red-and-white silk sari borrowed from Rashmi—red being the traditional color for women's wedding attire in West Bengal. To avoid the heat and escape the monsoons, the five-day weddings are usually conducted in January and February; some ceremonies are limited to the families involved. The wedding feast I attended was aglow with rich colors of both men's and women's attire and teemed with the sumptuous aroma of cumin and coriander mingling with sandalwood incense. Women's feet and hands were elaborately decorated in *mahindi,* elaborate designs painted with henna paste. Their jewelry was nothing short of regal. I even got to try my feet at folk dancing to the rhythm of wooden sticks that, like the other dancers, I beat over my head. To my amazement, I escaped unscathed. No matter what the social occasion or how elegant the surroundings, Rotarians coming together talked about their club's projects and how to do more in Calcutta to raise the quality of life for people there.

At the other end of the spectrum of life in Calcutta is Nirmal Hriday Manzil, "the abode of the tender heart," a hospice where the poor and destitute find refuge in which to spend their last moments. In 1995, when I was there, more than 40,000 people had been picked up from the streets and brought there to die. There, in blue-edged white cotton saris, woven at their home for

lepers, the nuns of the Missionaries of Charity carry out vows of
wholehearted and compassionate service to the poor. They oversee the home and the volunteers who come from around the
world to be a part of their work.

Carved over the doorway of a neatly kept brick building in
another part of the city it says "Let us do something beautiful for
God." Nirmala Shishu Bhavan is a haven for orphaned children.
As we toured the well-lit rooms, led by Rotarian Vijay Bhandari
whose Rotary Club of Calcutta did work there, children of all
ages clustered around us, reached for us out of their cribs, shared
with us their few toys. With plates in hand, some sat cross-legged
on the floor scooping out rice with their fingers or in a torn piece
of warm *naan*. It was there that I met a living saint.

Lucy in a jhoola in the home of
Rashmi and P. D. Tulsyan, Calcutta, India, 1995.

Sister Nirmala led us to the room where our two teams were to meet Mother Teresa. She directed me to the center of a semicircle of chairs. As Mother Teresa entered the room from behind where I sat, we rose. She came over to me and took hold of my hand, giving me to understand I'd been sitting in her chair. In that first physical contact, I felt the strength of her hands, a laborer's hands, yet endowed with tenderness to soothe the orphaned or dying. Swinging me around, she rearranged the seating, then placed me next to her. Sitting there with my hand fully and firmly in hers—except when she needed both her hands to illustrate a point—I was mesmerized. True to every account I've ever read, she radiated light. Even her hands, so calloused from scrubbing and cleaning and wringing mops, glowed as they moved. Her sandals were well worn, the bones in her feet misshapen from years of carrying her through long days of hard tasks. The sweater she wore for warmth had numerous holes darned with tiny stitches to make the garment last; she had a habit of giving away to those in her care the shoes or sweaters benefactors intended for her own use.

Her conversation was animated and passionate, the cadence of her voice musical, almost lilting. In a fine humor, she told us how hard it was to keep all her houses going, that we were lucky to have only one house that we were responsible for. She laughed easily at her own stories, as one would guess from the lines in her heavily etched face, and her laughter was contagious. It was hard to get a word in edgewise. Truth be told, would you interrupt Mother Teresa in the middle of a tale? I could not. When someone did, and asked where she got her inspiration and strength, she answered in one word: "God." When asked how she could care for so many people, she replied that she "talked people out of one handful of rice at a time" to feed those who had no rice. When asked what we could do for her, she told us to go home and do good there. Her eyes, whose clarity, not color, I remember, underscored her wisdom.

We were supposed to be with her for only ten minutes; instead, we were there more than an hour. As we got up to leave, she reached into a small box on the table, took a handful of silver-colored Virgin Mary medallions, blessed them, and gave them to us. She gave each of us her blessing in writing as well. Mother Teresa didn't take my hand when I reached out to shake hers as we made our way to the door. Instead, she put one hand on my forehead and the other on my cheek, blessing me as she pulled me down toward her face. The energy of that touch, that blessing, surges through me still, as does her challenge to "do ordinary things with extraordinary love."

After nearly a month of twelve-hour days consumed almost entirely by Rotary projects and events in Calcutta, and after our

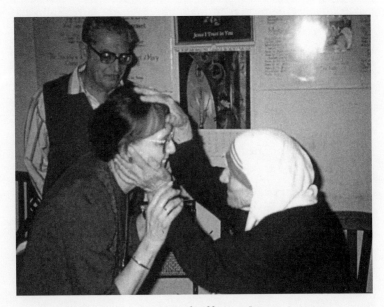

Mother Teresa giving Lucy her blessing, January 19, 1995.

Brazilian counterparts had departed for home, the American team got an unexpected break—a respite in the Andaman Islands. The Andamans, we marveled, was Eden in the Bay of Bengal. Tourist travel to many of the Andamans is restricted, in the interest of protecting aboriginal tribes and their culture. Yet by some blessed confluence of events, we found ourselves in Port Blair. Leis of fragrant tuberose welcomed us. For three days the five of us frolicked in the sea, stuffed ourselves to the gills with fresh, sweet giant shrimp, and saw the sights, including the ruins of British churches, homes, and a ballroom in the grip of pythonlike jungle vines on Ross Island, once the seat of British power. During the day I built sand castles with the children of Rotarians, and at night I saw constellations burning with a warmth I swear I could feel. At night, at Teal House where we stayed, secure under mosquito netting, I fell asleep to the ocean's rhythm and moonlight pouring through the windows.

On my last night on the island, I taught a group of Rotarian children my entire dance repertoire, "La Raspa" from my Mexican heritage and "The Chicken Dance" from my German background, both to melodies sung by their quick-study parents since I had no taped music. No plane on this trip had been on time. Rumor circulated that we might be "stuck in Port Blair" for an extra day, but the plane did come on the appointed day after all, to take us back to Calcutta for one last week of Rotary projects, presentations, and meetings.

On our last Sunday in Calcutta, my host and newfound friend Amitava Mookerjee took the team for a long walk through the streets of Calcutta. It was the first time we had walked any distance and mingled with the people living and working on the streets. He took us to a market where villagers were selling produce grown under the auspices of the South East Rotary Club, to which he belonged. We passed a funeral pyre tended by one man, the stream of smoke drifting over the Ganges, along which floated pallets of yellow and orange marigolds honoring the dead. We saw half- and all-naked children with sparkling dark eyes and tousled black hair playing unself-consciously on the sidewalk. Down at the ghats there were men freshly bathed with Ganges River water, wrapped in their clean dhotis, some getting shaves and haircuts and massages while they sat on the concrete steps.

The colors of the saris on the poor women in the streets were every bit as vibrant as the ones worn by the very affluent; their hand-embroidered shawls were beautiful as well. Every so often we passed a small shrine smack in the middle of the street where people stopped to receive their blessing for the day, the sandalwood incense and the scent of tuberose wafting out to mingle with the exhaust. And everywhere, everywhere, there were men and women with dots of sandalwood or vermilion smudges on

Men relaxing at the ghats after bathing in the River Ganges, on Lucy's last Sunday afternoon in Calcutta.

their foreheads in the third eye position so important in Eastern religions, as it is that eye through which the soul sees. I read in their faces a deep spirituality to which I aspire but feel certain will not come in this lifetime. That long walk on the streets was my farewell to Calcutta.

The next day we flew to Kathmandu, where Sabita Dakhwa, who was to come to El Paso as a member of District 3290 in April, served as our guide to Rotarian projects that focused on women in community development, and to the temples. In the temples, I lingered in the presence of Tibetan monks spinning prayer wheels that send the vibration of "Om Mani Padma Hum" into the universe. How can I describe standing at Nagarkot with the Kathmandu Valley below, watching the birds gliding open-winged on the wind currents with the snow-capped Himalayas as a backdrop? Or adding my lighted butter lamp to the hundreds glowing at the Buddhist Boudhananth Temple? Or flying in that small, white Everest Air high-winged plane along the mountain range all the way to Mount Everest? Mount Everest, whose foot stands higher than the highest summit of the Alps. I was there. I really was. On the walls beside my desk are two pictures: one of Mount Everest and another of me hugging the propeller of the plane in which I flew to see it. It wasn't that I was glad to be back on the ground. I did not want to turn loose, to let go of an experience I'd never have again, to let go of the wonder—the joyful and restorative powers of wonder.

On our own, following the completion of the tour, the Group Study Exchange Team flew that same evening to Delhi and in the middle of a cold night in a rented van made the bumpy ride to Agra. In midafternoon we toured the Taj Mahal, awed by its Mughal architecture of white marble inlaid with jasper, malachite, agate, lapis lazuli, bloodstone, and translucent carnelian. At sunset we watched the red sandstone of Agra Fort turn

Lucy hugging the propeller after seeing Mt. Everest.

bright orange. The next morning we returned to gaze at the Taj Mahal as the sun came up. Surrounded by dew-coated lawns and magnificent gardens, its ghostly image came into focus out of the darkness. With the moon still visible overhead, I sat spellbound as the changing sunlight took it from pale mauve through cream to a warm yellow. The sun's first rays touched the top of the dome, bathing it, then me, in first light. It was my last day in India.

At home I am closest to the experience of India when Tibetan monks come through town and I am able to offer them food or lodging. My father would have loved spending time with them. Most speak no English; they listen intently, though, and we communicate nonetheless. We speak through our eyes, our touch, through the sharing of meals, and meditations. There is communion. They have encircled my kitchen table chanting deep-voiced mantras that send vibrations of their devotion throughout my home. When they are here long enough to build an intricate sand mandala, I am especially grateful. To remind us of the impermanence of all things, they cut through the sand with a ceremonial *dorje* and cross out the designs so precisely created a few grains of sand at a time. They scoop up the sand, and together we go to where they can offer it to the Rio Grande, remembering there that all rivers are sacred.

Tibetan monk offering the colored sand
of a mandala to the Rio Grande

EPILOGUE

❧

RIVERS FOR ME are a continuum, linking not only each other but also past and present and most importantly all the people who belong to them and have touched my life. When I think of my rivers, I see my grandfather at the *Río Bravo*, my mother toddling beside him, helping him collect rocks for walls to surround the houses that he would build out of earth and straw, his legacy for his children. At the harbor of the River Elbe my father stands, blue eyes sparkling, young, strong, restless, waiting to embark on one adventure after another, that river taking him into the North Sea, then across the Atlantic to America, where on the Rio Grande he would find the love of his life. I see my mother, black eyes bright, wild ebony hair beneath a wide straw hat, her bare feet in the *Conchos*. There she is years later, her womb heavy with me, stooping to wash clothes in a stream from the Hudson River. She scoops up clear water to drink, to strengthen her for the climb back up to the cabin. I see her at eighty-one, still giving in to the temptation to let the trickle of any creek she encounters bless her feet.

In the trolley gliding over the bridge, I see myself, dressed in clothes handsewn by my mother, bows in my lime-juice-slicked hair, schoolbooks held close and a doll dangling from my arm. There are others watching with me from the Rio Grande as our sister cities, joined by geography, history, and culture, are shaped by the complexities of a new century. I see Johnny, my son, coming home to the crickets, throwing up his arms in jubilation to greet the summer rains, walking with his father in the arroyo, striking the pose of a beagle alongside the water that fronts the *Santuario de Chimayó*, collecting rocks at the many rivers we have seen together, standing tall at the Pont du Gard where centuries ago waters flowed.

There I am, wounded spirit and battered body, walking between hospitals along the River Clyde, smokestacks all around. Amidst the red sandstone buildings and thistles that line the sidewalks are strangers and new friends who hold and help me there, and a long way off are others, praying by my desert home on the Rio Grande. There's Paulette giggling at five-year-old Charles Emmanuel, who bathes unabashedly naked in the Dourbie River, while Fleur and Arnaud, his older siblings, watch and wait for their grandmama to serve us lunch. Together, Paulette and I dine overlooking the Aveyron River at Bel Castel, admire the Gardon River flowing under the Pont du Gard.

Hands pressed together, I salute the Divinity in the man who stands smiling in his clean dhoti on the ghats of the Ganges. Behind him rafts adorned in marigolds and tuberose carry the ashes of the dead downriver. In the Bay of Bengal, fed by the rivers of India, water splashes around me and stars warm me from above. As I fly along the snow-laden Himalayas, I am awed by waterways whose names I'll never know, far below. And on my last day in India, the Taj Mahal's splendor glistening in the distance, I see women washing clothes on concrete slabs along the Yamuna River. I see them become my mother—and every woman who has labored so along any river or stream.

I am thirsty for more rivers, rivers that lead me to other ancient sacred places, rivers to walk and cook beside, to sleep beside under stars not dimmed by city lights. I pray that rivers continue to bless me with friendships, joy, nurture, and knowledge, that they forever challenge me, and that they carry me back again and again to those who've made and make such a difference in my life. I want to emulate the flirtatious mischief of my mother, practice the life-embracing optimism of my father, and always, wherever rivers take me, to come home, here to the Rio Grande, which brought them together and gave me my story.

INDEX